WHEELER'S
FISH COOKERY BOOK

Mr Bernard Walsh, founder of Wheeler's

WHEELER'S
FISH COOKERY BOOK

MACDONALD HASTINGS
&
CAROLE WALSH

With drawings by
ANTONY WYSARD

London
MICHAEL JOSEPH

First published in Great Britain by Michael Joseph Ltd
44 Bedford Square, London, WC1B 3DU
SEPTEMBER 1974
SECOND IMPRESSION MAY 1975
THIRD IMPRESSION JUNE 1976
FOURTH IMPRESSION MAY 1977
FIFTH IMPRESSION NOVEMBER 1978
SIXTH IMPRESSION SEPTEMBER 1979

© 1974 by Macdonald Hastings and Carole Emmanuel

ISBN 0 7181 1238 5

Printed in Great Britain by
Hollen Street Press Ltd, Slough
and bound by Redwood Burn, Esher, Surrey

TO WHEELER'S CUSTOMERS
Everywhere

CONTENTS

(The asterisk denotes fish described with Wheeler's recipes. When there are no asterisks, the methods of cooking are generally identical with those for fish of the same family.)

INTRODUCTION   9

I   APERITIF   17

II   SAUCES   33

III   FRESHWATER FISH   43

*Salmon – Sea-trout – *River Trout – *Eels – Pike – Grayling Carp – Perch – Crayfish

IV   FLATFISH   59

*Sole – *Plaice – *Halibut *Turbot – *Skate – Brill Flounders – Dabs

V   ROUND FISH   79

*Herring – *Whitebait

*Haddock – Tunny – Sardines
Whiting – Mullet – *Mackerel
*Cod – Sea Bass – Conger
Dogfish – Hake – Bloaters
Sprats – Pilchards – Lampreys

VI   SHELLFISH   97

*Oysters – *Lobsters – Crayfish
*Crabs – *Prawns (Scampi)
*Shrimps – *Scallops – *Mussels
Ormers

VII   DESSERT   121

       INDEX   125

INTRODUCTION

It is a silly joke, cultivated on the Continent, that the English know nothing about cooking. In truth we are blessed with the best food in the world; and we know how to use it. We enjoy the real thing.

This book is about the real thing.

Nobody cares to give us the credit for it; but we have invented two meals, the splendid English breakfast and the charming English tea. We discovered bacon and eggs, devilled kidneys and Arbroath smokies. It was we who invented the cucumber sandwich, Gentleman's Relish, Dundee Cake; and from the East discovered the pleasure of China Tea.

It was we who married so happily roast lamb with mint, roast pork with apple sauce, roast beef with Yorkshire pudding, mutton with onions and red currant jelly. It was we who learned to serve boiled bacon with pease pudding; marinated mackerel and herrings with mustard. Jacket potatoes, buttered parsnips and Brussels sprouts, those lovely vegetables, are all our own. There are also those dishes which are so essentially English, like strawberries and cream for young women, ginger knob for youngsters, and walnuts and port for men.

English cookery, so much denigrated, is secretly the best in the world. The glorious net of fish which comes out of our Channel, and our northern seas, is incomparable. Fish from tropical seas are not bad. They are not quite as marvellous as fish which come from our own chilly waters. An Adriatic prawn is not contemptible. I like the red-fleshed fish of sunny seas. I like squid, its ink soup and the chewy bits of its tentacles. It is fun to eat an octopus you have killed with a spear in a trans-

lucent underwater wonderland. But the waves of the
Channel are the open sesame of a gourmet's dream.

There are bass in the white waters which I have
hooked casting a spinning line. Amongst anglers the
bass is the only fish in the sea, as the salmon is the only
fish in freshwater, which in the language of sport is
'killed', rather than landed. The bass fights on the surface
like the salmon. Most sea fish drive to the bottom.

But sport apart, and there is no better fish on the table
than the one who fights you, I have exciting memories of
catches in rolling seas of flounders, plaice, skate, dabs,
dogfish, conger eels and weavers. The fish that we hunt
are the best food that we eat.

I remember a dawn morning in the North Sea off Scarborough when I was trying to hook a tunny. We
ploughed a rowboat, put off from our Brixham trawler,
about the ringboats netting for herring. There were no
tunny; but the fishermen offered us a basket of herring
in recompense. When we got back to our own boat I
asked the skipper to fry one of the fat herring for breakfast. He told me that it would be no good until it had
had a few hours in the sun. By way of demonstration he
picked up one of the best fish and, crushing it in his
hands, reduced it in seconds, like a conjuror, to a palm-
ful of oil. The herring, that beautiful fish, needs time to
mature. As I shall tell you later, so does the salmon.

Although some fish are not on the regular Wheeler's
menu—people on an outing prefer the more expensive
kind—I haven't ignored them here. The herring, still
relatively cheap, has good claim to be numbered amongst
the most delicious fish that swim in the sea. I know few
accompaniments to a cocktail better than a winkle
hooked out of its convoluted shell. And I can think of
few things better than a tea of Morecambe Bay shrimps.
In my boyhood it would have been sprats. I also had a
taste—I used to fish them in a large rectangular net—

for sweet little brown shrimps which I collected at low tide between the piers at Hastings. When I was lucky I netted whiting too; and small eating crabs.

Making palatable dishes out of poor food is difficult. Making them out of good food is relatively easy. The experts will tell you that, in cooking first-class cold water fish, the less you do to it the better.

The problem is preparing fish for eating. Many funk it at a time when fishmongers, for economic reasons, are reluctant to do the work. But there is no reason why, with the right tools, you shouldn't do it yourself. While most of us would not wish to dismember a bullock or a sheep, even if we knew how, fish surgery is clinical, and can even provide a certain satisfaction of its own. Anyhow you had better make up your mind that, if you want to live well, there's a lot of it in the future you will have to do for yourself.

In the Brittany fish feasts it has always been that way. The shellfish is put on the table, with the appropriate cutlery, and the clientele are expected to deal with it. There is much to be said for the custom. The preparation of food excites the tastebuds. Eating is much the better for working for it.

Fish, of all food, decorates better than any other we eat. The presentation can so easily be a mouth-watering joy. For example I remember the patron of a small restaurant in the Dordogne serving freshwater crayfish with their heads tucked in a mountain of shaved ice.

It surprises me that so many people do not know the best way of enjoying fish after it has been cooked. Round fish, like trout and herring, should be split in half with the table knife from the back, exposing the backbone which can be lifted off to reveal the flesh. Flatfish are best handled with a draw of the knife down the backbone. The meat can then be raised off the bone on each side of the fish.

The fins on the edge of flatfish are a bony nuisance. It is best that they should be removed by the cook. It is normal to strip off the leathery upper side. It is wise with a sole, not a plaice, to remove the white underside as well.

A wide variety of culinary tools are produced for dressing fish. A cook in a good restaurant uses little more than a broad-bladed knife honed to a sharp point, with a fat grip and a good shoulder, a sort of hunting knife, which he works on a generously-sized wooden board.

A small kitchen knife, although you can get a sort of nutmeg-grater for the purpose, is good for scaling. A crusher of some sort, although the household hammer will do, is useful for breaking shellfish claws. In getting the meat out of shellfish I find that a miniature screwdriver, the sort you use on electricity parts, is invaluable. A curved chopper for pounding fish is a useful extra.

A luxury is a fish kettle, big enough to house a 15-pounder, for those who are fortunate enough to have a salmon river on their doorsteps or a good fisherman about the house. Nothing is better than a fresh-run salmon or a big sea-trout boiled whole. I sometimes think that cucumber was created to ornament this dish. In passing, a small cod, cooked in a fish kettle and offered on the table with a garnish of parsley, is squirearchical if not truly aristocratic.

Fish bricks for baking, and do-it-yourself smoking kits for trout, are readily available. But a keen knife, and a wooden board you keep exclusively for the purpose, are the essentials.

The cookery of fish should always be simple. If it isn't it is wrong. It is based on a knowledge of how to contrive a baker's dozen of essential sauces (see, importantly, pages 35 to 41). It rests, too, on recognising a fish in prime condition. The best rule is that it always *smells nice*.

The list in this book is not definitive. It simply includes fish from our own waters which are most likely to appear on the table. The recipes exclude those which should be cooked like others in the same family. The emphasis is on dishes served in Wheeler's, which are counted among the best in the world.

For practical purposes, the fish for which recipes are included are marked with an asterisk in the contents list. For example, there are twenty-eight ways of serving Dover Soles. There are no ways of cooking sardines, except fresh ones, because to cook canned sardines is a blasphemy. Nevertheless there are instructions here about how to mature them.

Throughout, even when no recipes are suggested, we have endeavoured to tell you how each fish can be cooked in the same style as others which have recipes of their own.

This is not designed simply as a book for the kitchen. It is also aimed to be something for the library. It tells how a tradition came about. Its intention is to whet your appetite before telling you how to satisfy it.

Myself, I am no cook; although I have a knowledge of fish on the fin. Carole Walsh, the daughter of Bernard Walsh, the founder of Wheeler's, has produced the recipes, helped with a know-how of which they have generously given, from the top cooks of all the Wheeler's restaurants. She herself became a Cordon Bleu cook in Paris at the age of sixteen. She worked in the kitchens of the famous London restaurant, The Ivy. She was in the Dorchester in London, and the Pyramid outside Lyon. She came to Wheeler's, and started the Soho restaurant, The Braganza. She was the entrepreneur of The George and Dragon, and, after producing a family, she acquired interest in the French Horn, that very expensive hotel at Sonning on the Thames.

If you follow this book carefully you can learn, without much difficulty, how to be a Cordon Bleu fish cook yourself. Meanwhile, an aperitif . . .

I

APERITIF

Books on cookery are supposed to be all about food. But good living is also about people. This one tells how people, many of them remarkable ones, created a legend. It was out of their taste, and their conviviality, that Wheeler's grew from a small oyster bar into an international club.

The original 'Captain' Wheeler is a shadow of a man who, in Dickensian times, had a shellfish bar in the fishing port of Whitstable at the mouth of the Thames Estuary. He was captain only in the sense that at some time or another he had commanded an oyster boat. It was a courtesy title conferred on the English Channel shores on anyone of mature years with a sea-chest and the sting of salt water in his complexion.

If Dickens had come upon him, during his excursions into Mr Winkle's Kent, he might have immortalised the 'Cap'n' as one of those larger-than-life characters who flourished as floridly as the moustache in Victorian England. As it is his only memorial is his shop which still survives inconspicuously in the old town. Like a blue plaque, commemorating some ancient worthy on an old building, it records what was; not what is.

Whitstable is no holiday resort. Its neighbour Herne Bay with its pier attracts the trippers. The beach at Whitstable is made of a mixture of mud and shingle which the locals call 'clike'. The small town has scarcely changed since, up to the nineteenth century, its industry was fishing; when a fleet of over a hundred brown-sailed yawls, crewed by bronzed men in blue jerseys, worked the estuary waters. Its prosperity belonged to a time when a member of the City of London's Corporation could report that the Thames abounded with salmon, large flounders, plaice, whiting, mullet, smelts, eels, perch, trout, carp, tench, bream, chub, roach, dace, and gudgeons, beside oysters 'of which these are the finest in the world'.

So they were. Ever since the Romans came, the oysters from the beds of Kent and Essex, of Whitstable, Mersea and Colchester on the port and starboard side of the river, were esteemed above all others. It is said that it was an indulgence for tribunes in the Roman army of occupation in Britain to have relays of runners to bring their ration of oysters to the inlana camps. It is a fact that even in the county of Berkshire, which is nearly as far as you can get from the sea in Britain, no Roman site is uncovered without the evidence of oyster shells among the ashes of the fires. Britain, as Tacitus wrote in his *Natural History*, may well be a misty island 'in which the soil does not afford either the vine, the olive, or the fruits of warmer climates'. But the harvest of its seas is matchless.

Way back, it is told that salmon were so prolific in the Thames that London apprentices used to have a clause in their indentures stipulating that they were not to be fed on the fish more than two days a week. While there are no documents to confirm that the indentures of the apprentices ever carried such a clause there is ample evidence that, up to the end of the eighteenth century, the Thames yielded such a harvest of salmon that it is only reasonable to suppose that people must have got fed up with eating them. It would be a matter for surprise if the apprentices didn't object.

In the Middle Ages, Henry III kept a polar bear in the Tower, given to him by the King of Norway, which he used to turn out in the river to catch fish for its meals. In the reign of Edward III the Thames fishermen presented a petition to the Crown to prevent farmers in the upper reaches reducing the stock of salmon by shovelling the fry for pig food.

The vanished race of Thames salmon was wiped out by an exploding population of Londoners on the banks of an increasingly polluted river. Alas, the oysters were reduced to a pathetic remnant, too. Pollution or otherwise, nobody really knows, a worm attacked the oysters in the Whitstable beds. The disease, which struck shortly after the Kaiser's War, had the effect of fragmenting the shell and killing the fish. Latterly, the great frost of 1961 temporarily destroyed the Colchester beds as well. It is also thought that that frost explains the almost total disappearance in large areas of the south-east of the red shrimps and prawns from the sandbanks and pools in the tidal rocks. English prawns, and what better, are a rarity now.

Yet I remember when I used to go out with my gins, skewered with a bait of crab, and bring back six dozen on a tide. As a schoolboy in the twenties I sold them for sixpence a dozen. The fishmonger resold them for a shilling a dozen. I hesitate to say how much you will be asked to pay, if you can get them, for English prawns today.

It is becoming difficult to remember—now that oysters (1974) cost anything in a restaurant from twenty-five shillings to fifty shillings a dozen—that, up to 1918, you could buy them from the beds in a handmade oak barrel for seven shillings and sixpence a hundred, with an oyster knife thrown in.

Fish, once the cheapest food in Britain, is now among the dearest. The scarcity value has been brought about only partly by natural disasters in tidal waters. Our seas are still lined with fish, as they always were. The difference is that modern methods of transportation have made them available to the world.

I know a pub in West Sussex, not twenty miles from

the sea, which is named the Lobster Inn. It is told that
it got its name from a time when a simple countryman
discovered a live lobster in the road; presumably an
escapee from a passing carriage. He believed it to be a
sort of dragon.

Until storage in sea-water tanks came along, the fruits
of the sea were only available within a limited compass
of their origin. Today there are operators, with storage
tanks of lobsters all over Europe, who can fly them in a
few hours to the area where shellfish are scarce; and the
price is booming.

The international market, with more and more money
to spend, is raising the price. The most expensive item,
in any top restaurant in New York, is a Dover Sole,
flown cost regardless from Billingsgate.

In the European Common Market we in Britain must
recognise that our native delicacies are likely to grow
more and more expensive. Our green grass grows the
most tender beef and lamb in the world. Our green seas
produce the most glorious fish, from the delectable
herring to the kingly salmon. Our fish are increasingly
precious. Even as the price goes up we should count
our blessings.

This book is to tell you how to make good use of them.
It begins, as it should, with the story of a stripling in
Whitstable some time towards the end of the First
World War.

Bernard Walsh, the founder of the Wheeler's that we are
all familiar with, insists that he scarcely knows his own
beginnings. But his background is carved into his frame.
He has shoulders on him which were built bending an
oar. He has the hands of a man who could bait two
hundred hooks laid on a long line pegged on the low-
water sands, and open a thousand oysters at lunch. His
boast is that, when he was a mudlark at Whitstable, he

could dig two thousand lugworms in a tide. At fifteen bob a thousand for bait (I am determined to ignore this new money which isn't money as we used to know it) he could earn thirty shillings in six hours work. In the age of the damnable P's you might call that about ten pounds spending power at the present time.

Bernard was clearly born to success. Perhaps the boy and the man is best revealed in his eyes, twinkling blue like things in the deep sea, sparkling with the joy of rockpools, rainbow-hued seaweed and anemones; eyes that always remind me of the look of crabs and lobsters in rocky crevices. It is true that men and women grow to look like the animals they love. Bernard belongs to the sea. In a sort of way the sea now belongs to him.

He insists that, although he was sent to school, he never bothered with it. He was much more concerned in helping his father in his fish business. He claims that he has no remembrance of learning to read and write. It just came to him as concert pianists tell that they cannot remember how they came to play the piano. Bernard remains a sort of mystery, one of those remarkable people who, out of nowhere, have influenced the society of their times.

I can think of others. There was Romano who, in the Edwardian age, attracted to his restaurant in the Strand some of the most amusing and brilliant journalists and artists of the old 'Pink-un' days. There was Gennaro whose custom it was to pin a carnation on the corsage of every woman guest in his restaurant. There were places like the Eiffel Tower where Augustus John, the painter, regarded it as his privilege to pinch the bottom of any girl who passed, and who paid his bill by making a drawing on the back of it. There was the Gourmet in Soho where Hilaire Belloc and G. K. Chesterton, their disciples about them, planned a new and now forgotten world.

In most of the memorable places the restaurateur
was an Italian or a Frenchman. Germans fell out of date
in 1914, Bernard was English ... well, almost.

His parents, who both lived to a great age, had their
origins in Waterford in Southern Ireland. His father's
business was in the oyster trade in Whitstable. His
grandfather appears to have been a horse-dealer who
specialised in producing matching pairs for the carriage
trade by the judicious use of dyes. Bernard remembers as
a boy driving a high-stepper. He remembers, too, family
talk of cock-fighting and bare-fisted boxing, the rough
sports of an earlier age.

But young Walsh knew relatively little of his family's
more disreputable activities. Indeed, apart from his
parents, he did not see much of his relations. His father
disapproved of relations on the grounds that they always
want something. Descended from a line of horse-copers
Bernard never learnt to ride a horse. But he could row
a boat with the best. He fished and he swam on the rim
of the Channel breakers. He laid his long lines on the
low-water mark. He learnt the trick of working a clap-
net. He poached oysters, beating the watch boats or con-
niving with them, when he had half a chance. In his
early youth Whitstable knew him, as they knew his
family, as another scallywag of the tidelines.

It seems absurd, but it is true, that the youngster,
when he grew into a man came to London, and became
an actor. He had been breeched in a world of oysters,
lobsters and crabs, whelks, mussels and winkles. He had
a passion for horses and horse-racing—that was a family
trait—an understanding appreciation of the animal plus
the fun of trying to beat the book. He coursed greyhounds and whippets on the track and in the field. Like
'Cap'n' Wheeler, who was said to have killed himself by
falling over his own gun, he enjoyed game shooting. Yet,
like Mrs Worthington's daughter, he went on the stage.

It seems to have run in the fish trade. His elder sister became assistant ballet-mistress at the Munich Opera House. The founder of another famous oyster bar filled the off-season by appearing in a pierrot troupe at Clacton. Bernard's father was a man of only five feet one and a half inches. Bernard, powerfully built and six feet tall, with those flashing blue eyes of his, earned four pounds ten shillings a week—no mean wage at that time—for two and a half years as a chorus boy and Assistant Manager, with occasional small talking parts.

It wasn't so surprising. There is a connection, which has persisted throughout the nineteenth century into ours, between the pursuit of the sports of the sea and the land, and the glamour of the theatre and the restaurant. The men hunting for the good life brought the two opposites together. In his brief stage career Bernard never lost sight of the oysters. Neither did he lose his love for the sport of kings and the laughter of Bohemian company.

He got a job in a show, which was a flop, in the West End of London. Many people at that time lost heart. The aftermath of the First World War was a period of appalling unemployment and depression. Bernard, married now, looked about for premises to start a wholesale fish business, and an oyster bar. At that time, premises weren't difficult to find. He had the offer, in streets lined with empty shops, of places all over the West End of London. He had a choice between Old Compton Street (£400 a year) and Jermyn Street (£500 a year). He settled for Old Compton Street where, by letting the upper floors, he could occupy the ground virtually rent free. He put up the name Wheeler's. His father, before he died, had acquired the title to it by buying after a brief tenure by another owner, old 'Captain' Wheeler's shop in Whitstable.

To start with Wheeler's (London) was entirely a

wholesale business. On the first day it opened Bernard supplied four and a half thousand oysters to top London restaurants. He dispatched them, as they were ordered, on two tricycles. Soon, it was caviare and foie gras as well. He soon realised that the Café de Paris, Café Anglais and the Blue Train, all fashionable restaurants of their time, were making a good thing out of his service. The Criterion Brasserie was selling six of his oysters, half a pint of stout, bread and butter, for one shilling and sixpence. From Old Compton Street he went into the retail trade himself.

He bought four tables at thirty-five shillings each and sixteen chairs for seven shillings and sixpence each from Whiteleys. Some of them are still in Old Compton Street today.

From the time he started in 1929, Bernard and his wife kept the oyster bar open, during the season, from 8 a.m. to midnight seven days a week. The price, for four grades of oysters, was two and six to seven and six a dozen. The best, which didn't sell, were Royal Whitstables and Colchesters. The cheapest, at two and six a dozen, nobody wanted. The bar flourished on greenbearded Essex at three and sixpence. Bernard himself, in a white jacket, dispensed.

I remember early days when I was a customer at Wheeler's. A small place in Soho, it was always crowded; that in spite of the fact that Bernard, like so many great restaurateurs, had his own rules about the right way to eat in his establishment. Potatoes were out. You could have oven-warm French bread and the best of butter. You had a choice of oysters, cold lobster and crab, smoked salmon, and when there was time to prepare the dishes, Coquille St Jacques, turtle soup, and Welsh Rabbit with parmesan cheese. Cheese rounded off the meal. Cheese, as much as you could eat, all at eightpence: Cheddar, Camembert, Gorgonzola and Stilton.

Bernard bought his Stiltons when they were made from the best June grass. He carefully turned them over every month until they were in their prime from November to Christmas, and beyond.

In one of the three star restaurants in France I remember the *maître d'hôtel* slapping a customer on the hand when he dared to add salt and pepper to his perfect soup. I recall a famous chop house in Fleet Street which, up to the thirties, refused to accept that Sir Walter Raleigh had brought the potato to the West. When Groom's, as it was called, finally accepted the fact of history, it sank into decline. To its customers, the introduction of the potato was the end. Thus Bernard, with an iron hand, preserved the integrity of Wheeler's. You weren't allowed to have what wasn't good for you.

Before the Second World War he slipped a little by hiring a chef to cook soles. The introduction was so popular that the people who came in for oysters before the theatre were pushed out by the people who came in for the Dover Soles. Determinedly, Bernard stopped the soles, and put a notice outside his shop: 'The demand for oysters prevents the sale of cooked soles.'

He was to change his mind, in different circumstances, later. But then, in his oyster bar, he had no occasion to think of what is now called diversification. He was making a good enough living to own a couple of steeplechasers. Out of the oyster season he returned to Kent where he had seaside shops, serving lobster and crab teas, cockles, whelks, winkles and the rest, at Margate and Herne Bay. He coursed his greyhounds in the field and on the track. He played golf on the famous Seasalter course at Whitstable; and won a prize for hitting a drive of 292 yards.

The war changed for him, like everybody else, his way of life. He served not as a soldier but in the world of secret not public service. The story of it is outside the scope of this book.

But throughout the war Wheeler's stayed open. Even after the bombs blasted the windows, and a cover of corrugated iron protected the inside, it was all warm within. It was always full, too. The mystique had been created.

In a battered London after the war, while food rationing was still in force, Wheeler's was a haven for knowledgeable gourmets. Fish, when it was available, had never been rationed. Bernard, back in his white coat wielding his oyster knife, showed the way to sanity again. Men who had just thrown away their battle-dress drifted back into peacetime living. Another era began.

Wheeler's, the sea in Soho, flooded with custom. It was still a bar on a ground floor which you could have ringed with a seine net; but it had a remarkable character of its own. Bernard, denying that he had any schooling, had a connoisseur's eye for what I can best describe as ichthyological *objets d'art*. He lined his premises with enchanting prints, paintings and china, a collection which I am sure will command fat prices in the salerooms for generations to come.

He also had an eye, to an extraordinary degree, for people. He showed himself one of those rare beings who attract others like a trout to a fly. Call the gift personality. Whatever it is it is the greatest gift that can be conferred on a host or a restaurateur. His customers wanted to know him.

Here I am in deeper water. I have to explain how Wheeler's, the little oyster bar, grew into a public company with restaurants, not just fish bars, all about the country. Bernard Walsh created the business. But I wonder, I just wonder, whether it would be all quite the way it is today if he had not attracted a group of colourful friends who appeared shortly after the war still dusting the austerity of those days out of their systems.

Bernard Walsh might well have been happy to stay with his white coat and his oyster knife, his horses and hounds, and his hideout in Whitstable. But the enjoyable world would have been a fraction the less fortunate if Old Compton Street had not been flooded by an unexpected tide.

The people most intimately concerned could never agree, even among themselves, on the origins of the Thursday Club. Subsequently, so much nonsense has been written, especially rubbish in American underground magazines, that it is good to tell the truth. *Life Magazine*, now defunct like the Thursday Club itself, offered large sums of money to learn its secrets. But there were no secrets.

The way it happened was that the then editor of the glossy society weekly, *The Tatler*, who had edited a forces paper in the Middle East as Lt Colonel Sean Fielding, an officer in a phantom army created to confuse the Germans, started a more convivial confusion in Old Compton Street. In the summer of 1946 he let it be known that contributors to his periodical who wanted to see him should not come to his office, but that he would be available every Thursday at luncheon in Wheeler's Oyster Bar. Thus the Thursday Club began.

Men of kindred spirit joined the informal editorial conference. As, each midweek, Wheeler's Bar became more crowded Bernard was tempted to provide a room for the company in one of the empty floors upstairs. It was a luncheon club which grew in the casual and great English tradition of the eighteenth century. In different times I am sure that Boswell and Johnson, and their cronies, would all have been founder members. The Thursday Club was born out of a sort of revolt after years of war in which we had all been bombarded with slogans such as 'Careless Talk Costs Lives'. It was a frivolity which our generation had been denied too long.

Making the rules of the club became a ludicrous game in its own right. It was early decided that the first object of its constitution should be to extend the British week-end from Thursday to Tuesday. An Honorary Secretary was nominated, called Charles Adamant whose address was 'Castle Granite, Outer Hebrides, N.B.' Some later members were fooled into believing that he actually existed.

During clothes rationing, while it still continued, we made an ebullient defiance against conformity by adopting claret-coloured waistcoats with gilt buttons engraved to a design by Antony Wysard, of the God Thor with his thunderbolts in one hand and a glass of port in the other. We had a pleasant custom of adopting a 'Champagne Charlie' for the day. In celebration of the wine, we sang the old music-hall song with such enthusiasm that Wheeler's rumbled with the noise. The Thursday Club is the only place where I have joined in drinking a rehoboam of champagne. The bottle stood as high as the table.

Yes, it was all nonsense; but so much of it was such witty nonsense. Some of the best storytellers of our time exercised their ingenuity at the table. Asked to tell the same stories again and again, they could win a cheer by introducing a variation in the form in which they last told it. It was a good association of men.

There was a book in which, each Thursday, members present, and their guests recorded their names and made outrageous comments on the week's news. The leather-bound volumes, extending from 1946 to 1969, are now hidden away. They are a unique record of the social and political history of our times. Whether any sociologist in the future can unravel them is another matter. Although I was one of the notorious Thursday Club, there is much that I cannot puzzle out myself.

Why notorious? I am blessed if I know. But somehow it got about that we had dancing girls on the table. We undoubtedly extended luncheon too long. After walnuts and port we were certainly in the mood to extend the British week-end until Tuesday. But our vices never extended beyond a riotous rendering of extracts from *Chu Chin Chow*.

The Thursday Club had different implications for Bernard. It must have been costing him a bomb to entertain people, albeit a lot of them very famous people, at a fixed rate, whose capacity for food and wine was remarkable. He himself admits that he loved the company, the glorious stories and the noise. But, let's face it, he was put upon.

One day, in the early years after the war, the members persuaded him—they had already conned him into laying on a 'Feast of St Bernard' every autumn at his own expense—that it was time to have done with cold food. They wanted something hot. Bernard got a Primus stove and cooked them a lobster soup, lashed with champagne, and anything else that came to his hand. It was really quite excellent.

The crackheaded Bohemians who had invaded his bar induced him to think twice. He learned from those men who wanted the best of everything. He had come upon a Chinese *saucier* chef, named Mr Song, who was clearly marvellous. Poulsen had employed him in the Café de Paris, and before that in the Kit Kat Club. Bernard found him out of the employment exchange. From then on, Wheeler's extended from an oyster bar into a restaurant and, due to the swell of customers, into a chain of restaurants. They are listed in a footnote at the end of this chapter.*

Antony Wysard, one of the founder members of the Thursday Club, contributed something of his own. A brilliant caricaturist and wit, he produced a publication such as had never been achieved before. Called *Wheeler's Review*, it has lifted a restaurant into the fine arts. Tony's magazine—illuminated with the work of the most sophisticated writers and artists of our time—travels the world. Wheeler's is so much more than restaurants.

---

* Wheeler's establishments now (1974) are: LONDON— Wheeler's, 19 Old Compton St, W1; The Alcove, 17 Kensington High St, W8; Antoine's, 40 Charlotte St, W1; Braganza, 56 Frith St, W1; Carafe, 15 Lowndes St, SW1; George & Dragon, 256 Brompton Rd, SW3; Wheeler's, 12A Duke of York St, London, SW1; Sovereign, 17 Hertford St, W1; Vendome, 20 Dover St, W1; Wheeler's City Restaurant, 19-21 Great Tower St, EC3. BRIGHTON—Wheeler's, 17 Market St, Brighton 1; Sheridan, 83 West St, Brighton 1. SEAFORD, SUSSEX—Wheeler's Golden Galleon, Exceat Bridge, Seaford.

II

SAUCES

(for Goose and Gander)

This is a brief chapter, but it is an important one. To be a successful fish cook, it is essential to know the way of preparation of a handful of sauces. If you know them you can compete with the *haute cuisine*.

FISH STOCK
1 lb. sole bones (or other fish)
½ lb. onions
2 oz. parsley stalks
¼ bottle white wine
juice of half a lemon

First Method: Melt a little butter or margarine in a saucepan and cook the onions without letting them brown or colour. Add the parsley stalks, fish bones and the juice of half a lemon. Shake the saucepan occasionally. After three or four minutes cover with the white wine and about three pints of water. Simmer for 20 minutes.

Second Method: Put the bones, parsley stalks, onions and white wine into the pan with three pints of water and simmer for 30 minutes.

ROUX
The roux is really the first thing to be learnt, whether at home or at the Cordon Bleu in Paris.

Here are the quantities for ½ lb. of roux, which is enough for one or two pints of sauce according to the thickness required, but it is very easy to vary the amounts.

4 oz. butter
4 oz. flour (but a little more butter than flour)

Melt the butter, but do not let it colour. Add the flour and mix. Let it bubble so that the grains of flour burst. If it is not cooked properly at this stage, all the sauces you make with the roux will taste of uncooked flour. Monsieur Augusti, who was the Chef at the Ivy, always put his roux in a low oven for 20 minutes. This gave it a nutty flavour.

BECHAMEL
2 oz. butter
2 oz. flour
1 pint milk
salt and pepper
nutmeg (if liked)

Melt the butter in a saucepan, add the flour and mix. Let it cook but not brown. Add the milk slowly and mix well until it thickens. Simmer for a few minutes. If you need to keep this sauce, put some butter on a knife and pass it over the top of the sauce, which will prevent a skin forming.

WHITE WINE SAUCE (VELOUTE) for fish dishes
2 oz. butter
2 oz. flour
½ pint fish stock
½ pint dry white wine

First Method: Make a roux. Add the stock, stirring constantly, then add the white wine. Bring to the boil and simmer for 30 minutes.
Second Method: Extra ingredients
sugar

cayenne
lemon juice
cream

Make a roux as above and add a very little sugar
and some cayenne. Add white wine, lemon juice,
the water in which you have cooked the fish, and
cream. Bring to the boil and stir until the sauce is thick
enough.

SAUCE MORNAY
2 oz. butter
1½ oz. flour
1 pint milk
2 oz. grated Parmesan or Gruyère cheese (or 4 oz.
  Cheddar)
2 egg yolks
2 tablespoons cream

Make a roux, add the milk and stir continuously until
boiling. Simmer for 5 to 10 minutes. Add the grated
cheese, stirring all the time. Beat the egg yolks and cream
in a bowl, just enough to mix them. Take the sauce off
the heat and add the egg and cream mixture. Re-heat but
do not boil.

TOMATO AND FISH SAUCE (Old Compton Street)
(a good substitute for lobster sauce)
4 oz. butter
4 oz. flour
1 small clove garlic
4 oz. tomato pureé
1 small onion
bay leaf
thyme
1½ pints fish stock (sole bones only) cooked with a bay
  leaf and celery

Melt the butter and add the sliced onion and crushed garlic. When brown, add the flour and let it all simmer a few minutes. Add the fish stock, tomato purée, bay leaf and a sprig of thyme. Simmer for half an hour, remove from the heat and liquidise or put through a sieve. This sauce can be kept in a fridge for 2 to 3 days. It can be laced with brandy and cream before serving and is for use if no lobsters are available.

LOBSTER SAUCE

3 lb. cooked lobster or lobster heads and claws
1 lb. tomatoes
1 tablespoon tomato purée
3 chopped shallots
2 tablespoons brandy
2 oz. butter
1 tablespoon oil
1 stock cube
parsley
1 clove garlic
tarragon
cayenne
½ pint white wine
salt and pepper

Crush the lobster heads and claws. Heat the oil and a piece of butter, add the shallots and garlic. Put in the lobster and flare with the brandy. Add the white wine and simmer a little. Add the skinned, chopped tomatoes and the tomato purée. Season with salt, pepper and cayenne pepper and add the stock cube. Simmer for 20 minutes.

Take out the pieces of lobster and strain. Add the parsley and a little tarragon. Thicken with flour and butter mixed, adding small pieces at a time until the

sauce is of the required thickness. Bring to the boil
once or twice.

HOLLANDAISE
3 egg yolks
8 oz. butter
3 tablespoons cold water
1 teaspoon lemon juice
salt and pepper
cayenne

Melt the butter, which should only be lukewarm. Place
the egg yolks and water in a thick shallow saucepan or
basin over a pan of hot water. Take care that the water
does not boil. Whisk until thick and foamy, remove
from the heat and beat in the melted butter a little at
a time. Add lemon juice, season with salt, pepper and
cayenne pepper, and keep lukewarm. If the hollandaise
should curdle, add 1½ tablespoons boiling water and
beat continuously until it comes back to smooth. In case
the sauce has to be kept, a little dry mustard at the
beginning or béchamel at the end will help to hold it.

MAYONNAISE
2 egg yolks
1 teaspoon salt
pinch of pepper
½ teaspoon mustard
1 tablespoon vinegar or lemon juice
½ pint olive or salad oil

Put all ingredients except the oil in a small basin, preferably a heavy one. Stir vigorously with a wooden spoon
or wire egg whisk. Add the oil drop by drop. It is
important that the oil should be at room temperature.
When the first half is blended the oil can be added more

quickly. Use more vinegar or lemon juice if it is desired to thin the mixture, or a little boiled water. Mayonnaise may be stored in the refrigerator if it is in an airproof container.

SAUCE TARTARE
½ pint mayonnaise
2 tablespoons chopped parsley
2 tablespoons chopped gherkins
2 tablespoons chopped capers

Add chopped parsley, chopped gherkins and chopped capers—about two tablespoons of each—to half a pint of mayonnaise.

MAITRE D'HOTEL BUTTER
3 oz. butter
the juice of half a lemon
salt and pepper
½ oz. chopped parsley

Soften the butter, then add the parsley, lemon juice, salt and pepper. Put this in foil and make into a roll about 1 to 1½ inches thick. Put into the refrigerator to harden and cut into slices as required.

SHALLOT BUTTER
(delicious with poached or grilled fish)
8 oz. unsalted butter
the juice of half a lemon
2 medium sized shallots finely chopped
salt, pepper, cayenne

Soften the butter without melting it, then mix all thoroughly. Serve in a fluted soufflé dish, or in individual pots.

GARLIC BUTTER (for grilled or baked oysters)
8 oz. slightly salted butter
1 oz. finely chopped shallot or onion
2 cloves of garlic, chopped
pepper
1 oz. chopped parsley

Mash well together.

LOBSTER BUTTER
1 oz. unsalted butter
1 oz. flour
the creamy intestines of the lobster and the roe

Put all together and mix well with a fork. This is used
to thicken and add more colour to a lobster dish.

N.B. *In the subsequent recipes, where these sauces are
used, salt, pepper and cayenne are omitted.*

III

FRESHWATER FISH

The best of the freshwater fish pass a large part of their lives in the sea. Salmon and, to a large extent, sea-trout fatten in saltwater. They return to freshwater to breed. Eels make a strange journey to the seaweed of the Sargasso Sea to breed just once in their lives. In due course, the elvers and some of the adults wriggle back, probably to the country and place of their origin, to fatten and feed on freshwater organisms. The females are biologically the big ones, much larger, as in many species, than the male. In bird life, for example, the falcon is three times the size of the tiercel. The true freshwater fish, of which the prince is the trout, can scarcely be reckoned in the same culinary terms as the fish which go to sea. River trout can be marvellous. The other true freshwater fish are, at best, tolerable.

SALMON

Salmon at its best is indeed the king of fish. At its worst, it can be quite horrible. Every cook and every gourmet should know the reason why. To 'read' a salmon, it is important to know the elements of its life style.

Salmon spawn in fresh water. To an uninstructed eye their fry look like small trout. The *parr* remain in the river where they were born, feeding like trout, until they are about the size of a sprat. At that stage of their cycle they put on the silver sea dress of a full grown salmon, and disperse into the oceans of the world. They are then called *smolts*.

Although it has lately been discovered that many of them work their way into the Arctic seas, others travel much shorter distances, staying away from their native rivers only for a matter of months before they return to spawn their own progeny.

These short term at sea fish are called in Scotland *grilse*. They usually scale about three and a half to four pounds. But others of their species stay at sea for three years or more. They are the big fish which can weigh anything from fifteen to fifty pounds. They are commonly called *springers* because they largely run home in the early months of the year.

It is questionable why some salmon go on distant voyages of exploration while others choose to hang about local watering places. It is a fact that a grilse of three and a half pounds can impregnate the eggs of a forty pounder. Whether their progeny will go to sea as unadventurously as an excursion to Brighton, or chance the deeps of the Arctic, is still a mystery.

One theory is what is defined as 'the law of divided return'. Since the level of water in fast-running rivers goes up and down like a drain it is thought that the fish, instinctively seeking the survival of their race, choose different times to run home. The notion is that if one can't make it up to the upper reaches of fresh water they have reserves to spawn behind them. I have seen fish on the east coast of Scotland, jumping mad on the tidelines when a drought was preventing them running upstream. Such is the pressure of the sexual urge.

All nothing, you might suppose, to do with cookery. And yet it has everything to do with it. If you know the ways of salmon you will know how to judge them for the table.

There are epicures who will only eat salmon when the springers are running early in the year. Yet a fresh-run grilse in June or July is also delectable, especially if it is a fish which has grown big on good sea feeding. A grilse is a poor thing smoked because there is nothing to carve.

For smoked salmon, which I shall discuss again, you want a side of one of the big ones from the spring.

If you have an angler in the family, salmon is the fish which will be brought most proudly into the kitchen. Every housewife should know how to assess it. There are simple rules.

A fish straight from the sea will be as moonbright as a sword blade. If you are a connoisseur you will look for the sea lice under the gills, creatures which soon drop off in fresh water. That sort of fish, with a great humpback, is the most delicious thing you can serve. If it has been freshly caught don't be in a hurry to cook it. New-run fish need about twenty-four hours before the curds in the pink flesh set firm enough to make the best eating.

From a culinary viewpoint salmon is the most pleasant fish to handle. It has a fragrant smell. Plunge a pointed knife into the vent, and run it up the length of the belly to the head. You will find nothing much inside. The reason is that salmon don't eat, except out of memory, in fresh water. Their viscera shrink. The great back is the fat on which the fish live in the madness of spawning. There is no difference in the eating qualities between a cock and a hen fish. Fresh-run fish, the cock with his beaked mouth, the hen with her pursed lips, eat just as well as each other. But there is a great difference between a fresh-run fish and a stale one. It is important to know the difference.

A fresh salmon, straight from the sea, is a silver bar curved in a beauty which reflects all the colours of the rainbow. With every week and every month in fresh water the colour changes. The fish grow sluggish. The great weight of flesh on their backs dries away. The silver tarnishes to red and black. Towards the end, just before spawning, salmon become uneatable. Much before that the fish, as food, are uninteresting. As *kelts*,

after they have shot their milt and roe, they are un-
speakable. Kelts which are caught in line fishing are
immediately released and sent, hopefully, on their way.
For a salmon, sex is miserable.

It appears that the fish in prime condition must be
taken only at the very hour that it runs from the sea
into fresh water. The Danes have recently caused much
controversy by netting salmon in their feeding grounds
in Arctic waters. They could only sell them in Middle
Europe where the taste in fish is middling. In that part
of the world they eat carp which is cotton wool with
pins in it. The salmon the Danes caught were not worth
consideration. The fish doesn't develop it's full firm
flavour upntil it runs into fresh water for spawning.

There is no doubt that the most splendid specimens
are taken in the nets at the estuaries of the great Atlantic
salmon rivers. It is worth adding, in case you didn't
know, that there are two sorts of salmon. There is the
salmon you get in tins, which has names like Sockeye
and the rest. This is Pacific salmon, a breed which floods
into the Western Coast of the Americas. It is netted in
huge quantities when it runs into the inland rivers. It
is edible, out of tins, in fish cakes and other diversions.
It is not salmon such as we are discussing here.

The Pacific breed is a weird sort of salmon, migrating
in warm seawater which, when it comes into the fresh,
dies immediately after spawning. Seabirds congregate
to gorge themselves on the carcases. Our own Atlantic
salmon has casualties, but a percentage of them roll back
to sea to grow fat and spawn again. Ours is a more
aristocratic tribe altogether. It is also unquestionable
that the Atlantic fish, at its freshest best, is the most
wonderful fish in the world.

Blessed with a new-run fish every cook should recognise that it is best cooked plain. Ideally it should be
steamed or boiled whole in a fish tin large enough to

hold it. On the point of killing it should be crimped, if it is not going to travel any further. With a kitchen knife, cut fairly deep incisions from the back to the belly at two-inch intervals below the head both sides. Hang up the fish by the tail to drain for ten minutes, then let it soak for a quarter of an hour in cold water, preferably in the river it was caught in. A crimped salmon requires cooking for only ten minutes, a little more if it is a big one, in boiling water, as the cuts enable the water to penetrate deeply into the bones.

Fish should not be crimped if they are travelling away from their home river.

In almost all fish cooking a knowledge of how to make a court bouillon is fundamental. A court bouillon is made in a bath deep enough to accommodate the fish which is filled, preferably, with equal portions of water and white wine; or even, if economy counts, a half glass of French white vinegar. Add chopped parsley, thyme, bay leaves, a few cloves, and a small sliced onion. Boil the mixture for about half an hour from cold, and then put the fish in. Simmer very gently. It is arguable that a court bouillon may be more satisfactory if it is raised to cook the fish from cold.

Most people only eat smoked salmon in a restaurant where, if it is properly presented with brown bread, it fill the whole circumference of the plate to the rim. But, often, people get sides for Christmas presents, and wives are landed with smoked fish after an excess of fisherman's luck.

It is expensive food and, for a home cook, it is important to know how to deal with it. The side of fish—a fifteen pounder will shrink by half—should be tacked to a board. Begin with a sharp knife by razoring off the crusty edges at the sides and on the face of the side of fish. If the fish has been gaffed there may be a bruised area in its midriff. Don't remove that until you carve.

Start at the middle, with the sharpest knife you have
got, and cut back towards the tail. If you are carving
as thinly as you should, you should see the steel of the
knife through the flesh. Arrange the slices, as large as
you can make them, on the plates, patterning them so
that they fill the plate. If any of the flesh is blackened cut
it out and put it on one side for further use. Smoked
salmon is far too valuable to waste a sliver of it. You
will learn its subsequent uses in the recipes.

But I am the commentator; not the cook. Salmon
come first because, in the language of sport, salmon
is designated as 'a fish'; just as partridges have the
exclusive right to be defined as 'birds'. Don't ask me
why. Perhaps it is just that they belong to an aristocracy
of water and land which is incomparable.*

POACHING SALMON FOR COLD SALMON
whole salmon
½ bottle dry white wine
few peppercorns
1 lb. onions
1 lb. carrots
bouquet garni
salt

Put all the ingredients in a fish kettle. Add cold water
to cover and bring to the boil. Cover with a well-fitting
lid and cook for 5 minutes very gently. Remove from the
heat and leave to cool with the lid on. This can take up
to 24 hours. Leave the salmon in its juice and use as
necessary. The salmon improves by being left in the

---

* It is a pointer to the future that (1974) salmon are now being
produced in pens, in seawater tanks in the lochs of Invernesshire.
The biologists are raising salmon, up to nine pounds and more in
three years. It is an experiment which is likely to be a foretaste
of fish-farming to come. These 'Marine Harvest' fish are delicious,
but they are not wild fish. A gourmet might mistake them for sea-
trout.

juice in a refrigerator for 3 or 4 days, when the juice turns to a thick jelly.

GRILLED SALMON
salmon steaks (one for each person)
flour
butter
salt and pepper

Dry each steak well, dip in flour and pat to remove the surplus. Brush with melted butter, season and brown both sides quickly under a hot grill. When brown, lower heat and cook for 8-10 minutes, depending on the thickness of the steaks. When done, the centre bone will move easily.

SALMON MEUNIÈRE
Choose good steaks and cook as for sole meunière (page 62)

DARNE DE SAUMON BERNARD
This particular dish was created by Wheeler's Braganza Chef in the sixties. It consists of classic seafish with a classic sauce, and is named after Bernard Walsh.

Cook the salmon in bouillon with a little wine vinegar and 2 slices of lemon. Make sure the bouillon does not come to fast boiling and, to prevent the salmon becoming dry, 10 minutes' cooking is sufficient.

To dress, lift out the poached salmon, take off the skin around the cutlet and set in the middle of an oval dish. Coat with white wine sauce and garnish with a lobster claw, blanched oysters, fried scampi and button mushrooms. It is advisable to surround the dish with duchesse potatoes (see page 53) decorated with a few slices of cucumber and tomato, which makes it much more effective on presentation.

SEA-TROUT
Fishmongers call them salmon-trout. I regret to tell

that, in keeping with popular vernacular, even Wheeler's call sea-trout salmon-trout on their menus. In fairness, in different parts of the British Isles, there are all sorts of local names for the fish. In Ireland they call them white fish; in Scotland, they are sometimes named peel, or sewin.

But they are still sea-trout (*salmo trutta*), fish which are close relations of the salmon, but which normally don't interbreed. They have the habit of drifting down to the estuaries after the spawning season to recuperate on a diet of sea food. They run upstream again, usually late in the year, to propagate their own kind in the upper reaches of the rivers.

I have caught sea-trout with tails like tarpon, running with shoals of mackerel in the sea. It is a curious fish which has never quite found its place in evolution between freshwater and salt. For an angler it is one of the best game fish in the world. Fished at dusk, which is the best time, the sea-trout fights like a fury. The courage of the fish is the measure of its culinary qualities.

It is my opinion that the sea-trout is better to eat than the salmon. The flesh is more delicate and light. The small ones, from half a pound to a pound, can be served as a breakfast dish. Bigger fish run up to eight pounds and, in favoured waters, much more. In pink beauty they are perfect boiled with a garnishing of lemon, cucumber, tomatoes and lettuce, accompanied perhaps with a few small new potatoes. Men, who have successfully fished for sea-trout, also drop a little tear of affection on their plates for their formidable adversaries as they eat them.

The small ones should be split across the back for grilling. It is probably best to remove the backbone before they are served. The larger ones can be treated exactly like salmon. Indeed, it is difficult, except for an expert, to distinguish sea-trout from salmon.

To be certain you must count the scales. No cook would wish to be bothered with that. Sea-trout is excellent served whole and cold with its head on.

All the recipes for salmon are good for sea-trout, so long as you treat them according to size.

RIVER TROUT

Trout are the sort of fish that angler husbands bring home. It is valuable to know where they caught them. A housewife can rely entirely on those sweet little brook trout—three or four to the pound—flicked out of west and north country streams. Wild trout make a perfect breakfast dish. But have a care for those huge trout from the southern chalk streams, like the Test, fattened on horse meat and released from the stews a mere week before they come to the fly.

I have hooked some of them. I have even tried to eat them. They were so awful as food that I buried them under the rose bushes. They killed the rose bushes. The members of the exclusive Houghton Club at Stockbridge have the good sense to leave the monsters they take out of the Test in the club refrigerator. There are good wild fish, which rise to the mayfly, in the Kennet. Feeding on freshwater shrimp they are as pink as salmon. The Galway coast of Ireland produces some good pink ones in parts of Loch Corrib, but not all of it.

What you must know is that brown and rainbow trout as a dish depends entirely on the river or lake in which they are caught. Smoked trout, usually rainbow trout grown in stews, is tolerable, even good. Fresh trout needs to be very, very good. The best are unquestionably the small wild fish taken from the burns and the becks. For obvious reasons you cannot buy that sort of fish in a restaurant or a shop.

In Wheeler's places you will eat the best salmon. The

fish are drawn out of the nets at the mouth of the river estuaries when they are in prime condition from the sea. There is no organised industry for trout; nor could be. Trout-fishing is a private affair. Commercially, smoked trout are worth anybody's money. Privately, fresh trout are an angler's perquisite. The smaller they are, the fresher they are, the better to eat they are likely to be. The more simply you cook them the better.

TRUITE AU BLEU

Rainbow trout are generally used for this dish. It is only possible to make it with live trout. Stun the fish with a knock over the head, clean them as quickly as possible, sprinkle liberally with vinegar and plung into boiling salted court bouillon (page 49). A few minutes' cooking will suffice. Serve with hollandaise sauce or melted butter.

TRUITE MEUNIERE

As for sole meunière (page 62), but do not overcook.

TRUITE GRENOBLOISE

For each person:
1 trout
1 dessertspoon capers
smoked salmon in strips
lemon juice
flour
2 oz. butter
a dash of oil
parsley

Dip the trout in flour, melt the butter with oil in a frying pan, and when hot put in the trout and add the lemon juice. When the trout is almost cooked, add smoked salmon and capers. Dish with a sprinkling of parsley.

TRUITE CLEOPATRA
As Grenobloise, but with soft herring roes and prawns instead of capers and smoked salmon.

TRUITE AUX AMANDES
Toast the almonds first, in a frying pan or in the oven. Cook as trout meunière and add the almonds before dishing up.

EELS
Even in Wheeler's, epicures enjoy smoked eels. On the Continent, especially in Spain, elvers, the baby eels returning to the rivers of their origin, are counted the highest delicacy of all. In England, they run up behind the Severn Bore. Locals with lanterns are waiting to scoop them out. On the bank representatives of Continental fish interests are haggling to buy the catch. You will seldom see elvers served in southern English restaurants. There is a demand in the north country. In the south it is perhaps an obsolete custom to eat stewed and jellied eels on Derby Day. But eel is one of the good fish which arrives, like salmon, from the deep sea.

EEL PATE
$2\frac{1}{4}$ lb. small eels
$\frac{1}{2}$ pint light beer or white wine
a handful of very fresh sorrel, parsley, chives, sage,
    tarragon and chervil, coarsely chopped
2-3 egg yolks
2 oz. butter
juice of 1 lemon
1 teaspoon of flour or matzo meal
salt and pepper
bay leaf
thyme

Skin the eels, cut into 2-inch pieces and stiffen in butter. Add the herbs, cook for a moment, and add enough beer or wine to cover. Season with salt, pepper, bay leaf and thyme and cook slowly until done. In the meantime make a thickening with the egg yolks, lemon juice, flour and a little water. Thicken the stock with this, heat gently but do not boil. Allow to cool.

EEL STEW
1¾ lb. eels
1 pint red wine
2-3 tablespoons brandy
4 oz. butter
2½ tablespoons flour
12 small onions
4 oz. mushrooms
slices of toast
a large bouquet garni
salt and pepper

Skin, wash and clean the eels. Cut into 2-3 inch pieces. Put in a pan with salt, pepper and bouquet garni. Cover with the wine and bring to the boil quickly. Add the brandy and set alight. Add a little water. Make flour and some of the butter into beurre manié, add and cook gently for 15 minutes. Sauté the onions and mushrooms in the remaining butter, and add to the stew. To serve, pour the stew into a casserole over the slices of toast.

PIKE

I remember lunching in the Tour D'Argent in Paris, looking down on Notre Dame, when Monsieur Claude Terrail, the proprietor, offered me a dish he wouldn't define. Under exquisite sauce I could not guess it. He subsequently revealed that it was Seine pike.

It requires all the skills of a great restaurant to make that bony, muddy water fish eatable. Whatever Isaak Walton may have recommended, whatever people in less fortunate climates may have to put up with, pike is not, as a table dish, for the sons of the sea.

GRAYLING

Grayling haunts most of the chalk streams. From pure waters it can almost be as good as trout. The snag is that it has to be scraped of its armour of scales. It is a dish for angling enthusiasts who like to eat what they catch. Fresh, it has a beautiful smell which is said to resemble thyme. Cooking it, follow the trout recipes.

CARP

The mirror, crucian and common carp are eaten widely in Middle Europe. The fish is a traditional Christmas Eve dinner in Vienna where I have stood up to my waist in them in freezing weather in stews in the Danube. Perhaps the Viennese cooks know methods that we don't know to make them palatable. The medieval monks cultivated them in stews in England; but that was before people in inland areas could get fresh fish from the sea.

PERCH

Perch from fast-running waters is said to be good. A beautiful fish to look at, I have never eaten it; nor, I think, ever will. No other coarse water fish is worth consideration; although I believe that the others are harmless unless one swallows an excess of their multiple bones. Follow the trout recipes.

CRAYFISH
(see page 111)

IV

FLATFISH

Off our coasts there are eighteen species of flatfish, some of them rare, all of them inhabitants of the sea-bed, and all good to eat. It is a matter of opinion; but the Dover sole, the halibut and the turbot are perhaps the noblest, with plaice a good House of Commons man. The dab, a plebeian though he may be, is worth his place in society.

SOLE

There are three sorts of soles. There is lemon sole, the highly coloured Scottish sole, and the grey witch sole which is taken on muddy ground in deep water. The Dover sole, fat and rounded, is taken in the Channel, the Southern Irish coast and further south, in the Bay of Biscay and the Spanish coast.

The French, with characteristic nationalism, like to call them Calais soles. There is no question that the Dover sole is one of the most beautifully edible fish that comes out of the sea. Never believe people who tell you that witch or lemon sole is the real thing. It isn't.

All the soles have thick hides. As a matter of taste you should require that the bottom skin, as well as the top, be removed. The fringe of fin-rays, which the soles use to propel themselves slowly along the sea bed in their search for food, is always removed when the fish is filleted. When it is grilled or fried on the bone, the fringe may well be left in the kitchen after cooking. It makes for a tidier plate.

Soles shoot their roe up to midsummer. They are

said to be in their poorest condition, for culinary purposes, in April.

Always buy 14 to 16 oz. soles. Skin on both sides and cut off the head and side fins if you wish. If the recipe requires the fish to be poached, trim the side fins after the poaching. Most of the following recipes are equally good served as whole fish or in fillets.

TO FILLET A SOLE

Take a 12 oz. fish and, with a sharp pair of scissors, cut away the fins on either side. Skin both sides by inserting a sharp knife at the tail end and lift the skin; pulling slowly, helping it all the while with the knife towards the head. Remove the head with a semicircular cut, leaving gut, which then can be flicked out with the knife. Cut down both sides of the centre rib, then cut away the flesh from the top end of the fish, outwards and towards the tail, keeping the knife close to the centre bone all the time.

GRILLED SOLE

Wash and dry the sole well, dip it in flour and brush with melted butter or oil. Put the sole under a hot grill which has been lightly oiled and cook for 10-15 minutes depending on the thickness of the fish. Serve on a hot dish garnished with chopped parsley and lemon.

SOLE MEUNIERE

It is always better to cook a sole meunière on the bone and fillet it afterwards if you wish. Skin the sole both sides and trim the fins and head. Flour the sole and cook in butter to which has been added a little oil and the juice of half a lemon. By adding the oil, the butter can get hotter without burning, and this gives the sole a better colour. When cooked (about 12-15 minutes) place the sole on a hot dish, pour over the cooking juices and sprinkle with chopped parsley.

SOLE MORNAY
One large sole per person
½ pint Mornay sauce (page 37)
2 oz. grated Parmesan cheese

Poach the soles in a stock made of fish bones, onions and carrots and a little white wine. Heat the sauce and pour it over the cooked fish, sprinkle with grated cheese and brown quickly under a hot grill. Serve with piped mashed potatoes, which may be bound with a whole egg to make them firmer. They are then called duchesse potatoes.

SOLE VERONIQUE *(fillets or whole soles)*
1 large sole per person
½ pint delicate white wine sauce (preferably made with Sauterne) (page 36)
muscat grapes
2 tablespoons double cream
water or fish stock seasoned with salt and pepper

Poach the sole. When cooked, remove side bones, head and tail. Add 2 tablespoons of double cream to the hot wine sauce but do not boil. Cover the sole with the sauce and decorate with cold skinned grapes.

SOLE MARGUERY
1 large sole per person
4 oz. peeled prawns or shrimps
4 oz. shelled mussels (page 113)
4 oysters
3 whole mushrooms
2 tablespoons double cream
½ pint white wine sauce (page 36)
salt and pepper
water or fish stock

Poach the sole. Blanch the mushrooms, mussels and oysters. To the hot wine sauce add prawns, mussels, oysters, cream and extra seasoning to taste. Cover the sole with the sauce and decorate with the mushrooms.

SOLE NORMANDE
1 large sole per person
½ pint white wine sauce (page 36)
2 deep-fried scampi
2 button mushrooms, cooked in butter
1 lobster claw, poached
fish stock

Poach the trimmed sole in the fish stock. Cover with the sauce, garnish with the scampi, mushrooms and lobster and finish under the grill.

SOLE MAISON (Wheeler's, Duke of York Street)
1 large sole per person
½ lb. large fresh tomatoes or one tin of tomatoes
¼ lb. sliced mushrooms
2 tablespoons chopped parsley
1 saltspoon of sugar
1 chopped shallot
salt and pepper

Poach the sole in water or fish stock and white wine with salt and pepper. While it is cooking, boil the whole tomatoes for 4-5 minutes, remove their skins and chop them into pulp. Cook the pulp with butter, shallot, sugar and mushrooms for 10 minutes. Pour the tomato mixture over the fish and finish with chopped parsley.

FILLETS OF SOLE POMMERY or SOLE POMMERY
1 large sole per person
4 oz. butter

1 dessertspoon oil
1 large eating apple, peeled and sliced
juice of half a lemon
mango chutney
flour
salt and pepper

Dip the sole in flour and also the slices of apple. Melt
the butter and add the oil. When hot, put in the sole
and cook until nicely brown. Sprinkle with lemon juice
and chopped parsley. Add the apple slices two minutes
before the sole is cooked, but do not touch them while
cooking as they will break easily. The exact time for
cooking the apples depends on the type. Arrange the
sole on a dish and decorate with the apple. Serve the
chutney separately.

SOLE CAPRI
As above, substituting bananas for apples.

SOLE ST GERMAIN
Grilled sole with breadcrumbs and maître d'hôtel butter
(see page 40) added after it is cooked. Put under the
grill again until the butter has melted.

SOLE ANTOINE
1 sole per person
4 oz. butter
2 artichoke hearts, tinned will do
2 oz. prawns
2 tablespoons hollandaise sauce (page 39)
a little lemon juice
salt and pepper

Skin the sole on both sides and dip in flour. Melt the
butter and cook the fish as for sole meunière. While
the fish is cooking, prepare the artichoke hearts. Make

c

the hollandaise and add the prawns to it. When the sole is cooked, put it on a dish, fill the artichoke hearts with the hollandaise and prawns. Place the stuffed artichokes on top of the fish, allow to warm through and serve.

SOLE EGYPTIENNE
1 sole per person
1 aubergine
2 oz. mushrooms, finely chopped
2 oz. onions, finely chopped
½ pint white wine sauce (page 36)
2 tablespoons lobster sauce (page 38)

First of all get ready the white wine sauce and lobster sauce. Grill the aubergine or fry it in oil and scoop out the inside, removing the pips if you can. Lightly cook the mushrooms and onions in butter, add these to the aubergine. Poach the sole, stuff the aubergine, onion and mushroom mixture into the skin of the aubergine and arrange all on a dish. Cover the sole with white wine sauce and finally the lobster sauce in a circle. Put under a grill to glaze.

SOLE ALCOVE
1 large sole per person
4 oz. butter
oil
the juice of half a lemon
2 oz. prawns
2 oz. sliced mushrooms
1 small slice smoked salmon
2 tablespoons white wine sauce (page 36)
1 tablespoon chopped parsley

Skin the sole on both sides but do not cut off the head. Dry it. With a sharp knife, make a cut on the thick side as if you were going to fillet it, but cut only enough to allow the fillet to be rolled back. Cut through the backbone at each end so that it can be removed easily when the fish is cooked. Dip the sole in flour.

Put the butter in a frying pan with a dash of oil and cook as for sole meunière.

When the sole is almost cooked, put the white wine sauce in a pan and heat it with the mushrooms and prawns. Slice the smoked salmon into small strips and mix well. Add pepper and a little lemon juice. Fill the opened back of the cooked sole with the mixture and sprinkle with parsley.

SOLE MARYLAND
1 large sole per person
½ pint white wine sauce (page 36)
1 tomato
4 asparagus tips
1 slice of truffle
1 tablespoon double cream

Make the white wine sauce. Cut the tomato in half and grill. Poach the sole. Add the cream to the sauce, pour over the sole and decorate with the asparagus tips, tomato and truffle.

SOLE WALEWSKA
1 large sole per person
slices of lobster
½ pint Mornay sauce (page 37)
2 oz. grated cheese

Make the Mornay sauce and poach the sole. Place the slices of lobster down the centre of the sole, cover the fish with the sauce, sprinkle with grated cheese and put under the grill to glaze.

SOLE CUBAT
1 large sole per person
½ pint Mornay sauce (page 37)
½ glass of sherry
½ lb. mushrooms
small knob of butter
slice of truffle
2 tablespoons brandy

Make the Mornay sauce and poach the sole. Chop the mushrooms and truffle finely and put them in a small saucepan with a knob of butter. Simmer these for three minutes, then add the brandy and set alight for a moment. Lay the mushroom mixture in a dish as a bed for the sole. Add sherry to the Mornay sauce and pour it over the fish. Sprinkle with cheese and brown under the grill.

FILLETS OF SOLE FLORENTINE
1 large sole per person
¼ lb. cooked leaf spinach
½ pint Mornay sauce (page 37)
2 oz. grated Parmesan cheese

Poach the sole, place on a bed of leaf spinach and cover with Mornay sauce. Sprinkle with cheese and put under a hot grill for a few minutes to brown.

SOLE SOVEREIGN
1 large sole per person
¼ lb. tomatoes
¼ lb. mushrooms
1 slice of truffle
3 asparagus tips
½ pint white wine sauce (page 36)
salt and pepper

Poach the sole. Skin the tomatoes, remove the seeds and dice the flesh. Put into a small saucepan to warm. Add salt and pepper. Slice and blanch the mushrooms. Cook the asparagus if fresh, warm if tinned or frozen.

When the sole is cooked, add the mushrooms to the white wine sauce and cover the sole. Put the tomato at one end of the fish, the asparagus tips at the other end, and the truffle in the middle. Sole Sovereign is very nice served with mashed potatoes round the dish.

SOLE PORTUGUAISE
1 14-16 oz. sole per person
½ lb. large fresh tomatoes or a 1 lb. tin of tomatoes
1 medium sized shallot (chopped)
1 tablespoon chopped parsley
½ teaspoon sugar
salt and pepper

Poach the sole and, while it is cooking, chop the tomatoes. Put a knob of butter in a pan, add the chopped shallot and tomatoes, ½ teaspoonful of sugar, salt and pepper. Cook for 10 minutes. When the sole is cooked, cover with the tomato sauce and sprinkle with chopped parsley.

SOLE COLBERT
1 14-16 oz. sole per person

Skin the sole but do not cut off the head. Clean and dry and make a cut on the thick side as if you are going to fillet it, but only cut enough to allow the fillet to be rolled back. Cut through the bones so that they can easily be taken out when cooked. Leave the fillets rolled back, dip in flour, then in beaten egg, and then in breadcrumbs. Fry in deep, hot fat for 8-10 minutes. Drain well, remove the bone from between the fillets, and fill the hollow with maître d'hôtel butter, see page 40.

FILLETS OF SOLE BONNE FEMME (3 people)

3 14-16 oz. soles
1 pint white wine
½ lb. mushrooms
hollandaise made with 2 egg yolks and 6 oz. butter
parsley
2 tablespoons thick cream
1 oz. finely chopped shallots

Arrange the fillets in an oval fireproof dish, sprinkle with the chopped shallots, season and poach in the white wine with an equal amount of fish stock for 15 minutes. Slice the mushrooms and add to the fish stock. Remove the fillets. Reduce the stock until there is almost nothing left, then add the hollandaise sauce, the cream and the chopped parsley. Coat the fillets and put them under a hot grill to glaze.

SOLE CARDINAL

1 large sole per person
½ pint lobster sauce (page 38) or tomato and fish sauce
  (page 37)
2 tablespoons brandy
4 button mushrooms
knob of butter
1 lobster claw, cooked

Make the sauce and add the brandy. Poach the sole and warm the claw of lobster. Cook the mushrooms in a knob of butter and a little lemon juice. When the sole is cooked, place the claw on top and cover with the sauce. Decorate with the mushrooms. Grill for a minute or two.

SOLE GRAND DUC (Wheeler's 'Sole Gondu')

1 large sole per person
4 asparagus tips

½ pint Mornay sauce (page 37)
2 oz. grated cheese

Poach the sole, cover it with the sauce and decorate
with asparagus tips. Sprinkle with grated cheese and
brown under the grill.

GOUJONS OF SOLE
Cut fillets of sole diagonally, dip in flour and beaten
egg and milk, and finally in breadcrumbs. Fry in deep
hot oil and serve with tartare sauce (page 40).

SOLE DIEPPOISE
1 large sole per person
½ pint white wine sauce (page 36)
¼ lb. sliced mushrooms
2 oz. shrimps
2 oz. mussels

Poach the sole, and make the white wine sauce. Blanch
the mushrooms. Add them with the shrimps and mussels
to the sauce. A tablespoonful of cream may be added if
if you wish. Glaze under a grill.

SOLE PALACE
1 large sole per person
¼ lb. sliced mushrooms
1 tablespoon chopped parsley
4 cooked skinned tomatoes (fresh or tinned)
4 asparagus tips (tinned, fresh or frozen)
½ pint white wine sauce (page 36)
water or fish stock

Poach the sole. Make the sauce hot and add sliced mushrooms and parsley, followed by the cream. Pour the
sauce over the cooked sole, garnish with asparagus and

chopped tomato. Finish under the grill for two minutes to glaze.

SOLE FRANCAIS
A simple version of the above. The poached sole is covered with white wine sauce enriched with cream and decorated with asparagus tips.

SOLE DUBARRY
1 large sole per person
¼ pint white wine sauce (page 36)
¼ pint lobster sauce (page 38)
water or fish stock

Poach the sole in the stock and trim off side bones, head and tail. Cover half the fish with wine sauce and half with lobster sauce. Glaze under the grill.

PLAICE
The flatted plaice, with its relations, is among the more important fish foods of the North Sea. Plaice are the most beautifully adapted to their way of life of all the groups of bottom-living fish. Sir Alister Hardy expresses it well: 'The plaice is so modified that it lies on the bottom on its left side with its right side uppermost. Its head is remarkably twisted so as to bring both its eyes on to the upper and right hand side, and the margins of the body are provided with continuous fins. The original right side of the body—the "upper side"— is dark and dappled with red spots; the left, or "under side", lacks pigment and is white. The plaice swims by undulating its flat body in a series of waves passing from head to tail, and so skims horizontally forward like a billowing magic carpet. After swimming for a short distance a little above the bottom, it glides down to

come to rest again. As it settles, it wiggles its marginal
fins, so that they throw up a shower of sand or fine gravel
to fall upon its edges and thus obliterate its outline.'

I quote what he tells about the undulating movement
of the plaice on the sea bed because it is a vice of our
times not to know the ways of the animals that we are
eating. They are not things that come out of packets.
We live on their lives. It is of course necessary that we
must use them to feed ourselves. But we should do it
with respect, and knowledge. The plaice is at its best
for the table from May to January.

With the characteristic red spots on its back, it is
one of the best fish that comes from our seas. Unlike
the soles, which should be stripped of their skins, under
side as well as top side, the under side of plaice is too
delicate to trim. Its culinary presentation is much the
same as sole.

PLAICE HAMBURG
Elizabeth Ray has provided this recipe, which she tasted
in the Maternus restaurant in Bad Godesberg. The
method of cooking is plain enough, but the bacon garnish gives extra interest to this rather soft-textured fish.
At Maternus it is also garnished with shrimps, which
are delicious, but prawns or frozen shrimps will not do,
so if you can't find the real thing, leave them out.

2 plaice
lemon
salt and pepper
flour
3 rashers streaky bacon
1 small onion
parsley
fresh shrimps

Wash and dry the fish, then rub over well with the cut

side of a lemon, sprinkle with salt and pepper, and dip into flour to coat it. Chop into very small dice three rashers of streaky bacon (for two plaice) and a small onion and cook together slowly until the onion is soft and the fat has run from the bacon. Add a tablespoon of chopped parsley. In a separate pan fry the plaice on both sides until cooked through and golden in colour. Put on to a serving dish with the garnish of bacon and onion (and shrimps, if available) spread on top. Serve with a wedge of lemon and plain boiled potatoes. This dish is usually made with whole fish on the bone, but fillets can be used; the same garnish can, of course, be used to cheer up any other white fish.

PLAICE DIANA
4 fillets of plaice
$\frac{1}{4}$ *lb. mushrooms*
$\frac{1}{4}$ *lb. onions*
a few fresh breadcrumbs
parsley
1 egg
salt and pepper
lemon juice

Finely chop mushrooms, onion, parsley and breadcrumbs and mix with an egg, salt and pepper. Spread the stuffing thickly on the plaice, roll up the fillets and pack them into a buttered fireproof dish. Put a knob of butter on each fillet add a squeeze of lemon juice, cover the dish and bake in a moderate oven for 20 minutes. Serve sprinkled with parsley.

HALIBUT
The ideal size for a halibut, which produces such excellent steaks, is said to be about three pounds; although

Sir Alister Hardy records that the biggest, landed at Hull, scaled just on forty stone (560 lb.) At that weight it was valuable only for the unpalatable, although popularly therapeutic, liver oil. I recollect a Norwegian at Hammerfest, the most northerly town in the world, drinking it as pleasurably as a dry martini. For the rest of us this huge flatfish is best served in its youth.

Halibut, like turbot, can be cooked whole, but it is more usual for it to be served in slices.

POACHED HALIBUT

Put the fish in cold fish stock with a little lemon juice and bring to the boil slowly. Simmer for 10-12 minutes.

Serve with hollandaise sauce, or with a sauce béchamel with chopped capers and hard-boiled eggs.

HALIBUT AU BEURRE NOIR

Dip the slices of halibut in flour and fry in butter. When cooked, remove the fish. Add chopped parsley and a few drops of vinegar to the butter. Pour this over the fish and serve with boiled or creamed potatoes.

HALIBUT BRISTOL

For 2 people:
2 slices of halibut
$\frac{1}{2}$ doz. oysters
2 oz. grated cheese

Poach the halibut in salted water with a little milk added. Make $\frac{1}{2}$ pint of béchamel, add the yolk of one egg and two tablespoons of double cream. The $\frac{1}{2}$ doz. oysters just bring to the boil in slightly salted water. When the fish is cooked, place on a dish, cover with the cream sauce and decorate with the oysters. Sprinkle with cheese and brown under the grill.

TURBOT

This is one of the large flatfish, shaped like a heart. It is best served in steaks. Its full flavour responds to all the arts of cooking. It is best in summer, and is usually very expensive.

Like halibut, it is usually served sliced, about 6-8 oz. a person.

POACHED TURBOT (HOLLANDAISE)

Put the fish in cold fish stock with some slices of lemon. Bring slowly to the boil and simmer.

For a whole fish ($1\frac{1}{2}$ to $1\frac{3}{4}$ lb.) allow 30 minutes, but for 2 or $2\frac{1}{2}$ lb. allow only 40 minutes. If you are poaching a slice, it will take 8-10 minutes, depending of course on the thickness of the slice.

Another way of poaching turbot is in salt water with milk added to it.

FRIED TURBOT

6-8 oz. slices

Wash and dry the fish and dip in seasoned milk, then in flour, and fry in deep hot oil for 8-10 minutes. Serve with lemon and tartare sauce.

Or Wash and dry the fish and dip in milk with a beaten egg, then in fresh breadcrumbs. Fry in hot oil.

TURBOT MORNAY (Slice)

Poach the turbot in fish stock for 8-10 minutes. Make $\frac{1}{2}$ pint Mornay sauce per slice. Put the fish on a dish, cover with sauce and sprinkle with grated cheese, then brown under the grill.

GRILLED TURBOT

If you are going to cook a whole fish, score it on both sides, brush with oil and grill in the usual way.

If you are grilling a slice of turbot, it will take about

10 minutes for a slice 1 in. thick. This can be served with melted butter, béarnaise sauce or shallot sauce.

17th-CENTURY RECIPE

This recipe comes from a Japanese, Shizou Tsuji, who runs a large catering school in Osaka.

Take a slice of turbot, put it in a shallow dish and cover it with cream. Add salt and pepper and simmer very gently for 12-15 minutes. Take the fish out of the dish, reduce the cream, add the yolk of an egg and lemon juice, and beat until it becomes thickened. Place the fish on a dish and cover with the sauce. Fish cooked this way remains very moist.

TURBOT AU CHAMPAGNE

Cut the fish in slices and put into a buttered frying pan with freshly skinned and chopped tomatoes. Moisten with champagne and freshly chopped parsley. Leave to simmer for 10 minutes.

Take out the fish and reduce the sauce until it has thickened. Add a ladle of fresh cream. Season and cover the turbot with the sauce.

SKATE

The skate is in some ways a weird fish. It is one which, when the Scandinavians hang it up on the line to dry, is never attacked by blowflies. I have eaten sting rays, in all manner of peculiar circumstances, about the world. The wings, which are not bone but a soft fatty substance, are counted a delicacy.

SKATE AU BEURRE NOIR

1 wing of skate (1½ lb. or more)
fish stock (page 35)
2 oz. butter

2 *tablespoons wine vinegar*
1 dessertspoon capers
salt and pepper
chopped parsley

Trim the skate and cook it very slowly in the fish stock for 25 minutes. Drain the pieces and tidy away the skin. Keep them hot in a dish.

To make the beurre noir, cook the butter gently until it is brown. Pour this over the fish. In the butter pan, cook the vinegar quickly to reduce it. Add this to the fish with capers and parsley.

Skate may also be fried or poached and served with a hollandaise sauce (page 39).

BRILL
A big flatfish, not unlike the turbot in appearance but unworthy of the turbot in flavour. It is the sort of fish which needs a good sauce. It is rather uncommon in British waters.

FLOUNDER
The flounder is a sort of plaice which flourishes not only in the sea but in the brackish waters of river estuaries. Cats love it.

DABS
Dabs, the delight of inshore anglers, have no place in the commercial market. Sweet little flatfish, similar to plaice and flounders, they are ideal for breakfast or tea, steamed, boiled, fried or baked. Like sprats, with other lesser fish within the law, they are delicious. It is curious that they are a separate species from other flatfish out of the sea. They look like the young of larger fish.

They may be cooked like soles or plaice. But they are better plain grilled, or fried.

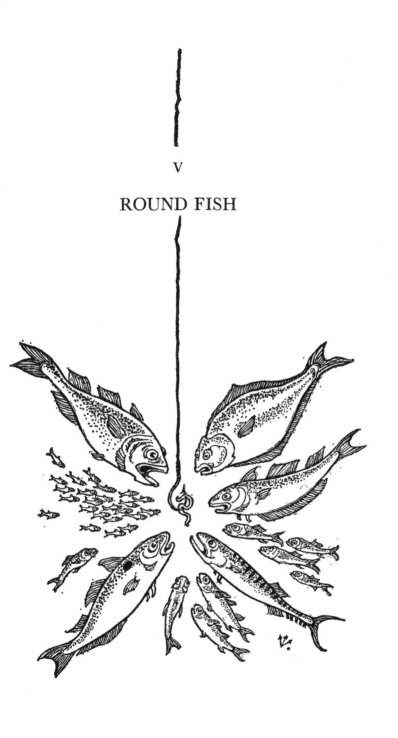

V

ROUND FISH

The fish harvest off our coasts is largely round fish, those animals which feed in the surface waters. They use the food of the sea as cattle graze grass. They feed on living organisms, the plankton, which clothe the sea like vegetation on the land. The plankton is largely composed of baby fish. In the balance of nature a certain cannibalism is what makes it work.

HERRING

The herring is the most plentiful fish in our nothern seas. Some shoals are said to be eight or nine miles in length and two or three miles in breadth. The great Victorian biologist, T. H. Huxley, who was sometime Fishery Inspector, estimated that the shoals of fish, in the seasons in which they swam together 'are closely packed, like a flock of sheep straying slowly along a pasture, and it is probably quite safe to assume that there is at least one fish for every cubic foot of water occupied by the shoal. If this be so, every square mile of such a shoal, supposing it to be three fathoms deep, must contain more than 500-millions of herring.'

As each herring lays at least ten thousand eggs, the multiplication table is a subject for the wildest arithmetical calculations. The other denizens of the deep, especially the haddock, feed on the spawn. Man draws an enormous harvest of the ripe fish. Nature, so abundant, possibly deemed that it should be so.

At a time when oysters were a Cockney dish the rich disowned them. While herrings are still relatively cheap —and they may well become very expensive if over fishing gets much worse—we should be making the most of them. They are the richest food that the fishermen bring to us. They too live on the plankton, that extraordinary accumulation of phosphorescent surface life in the oceans of the world which is as wide or wider in its variety as the plant species we list on the third of the world we occupy, the land. The herring, like most fish, are the cattle of a vegetation other than our own.

The season of the herring varies on different parts of our coasts. The spent fish, when they have shot their eggs and their melt, are the poorest for the table. Herrings are best at their biggest, when they are probably about five years old. You can eat them so many ways.

Soft roes on toast are the perfect savoury. Salted herring, like Bismarck herrings with onions, are admirable as an introduction to food after a hangover. With a little Worcestershire sauce, to give an edge to the tooth, they will restore the most jaded appetite.

FRIED HERRINGS
Dip the herrings in flour, then egg and breadcrumbs, and deep fry. Serve with lemon and fried parsley.

HERRING MEUNIERE
Score the herrings on both sides and dip in flour. Fry in melted butter with a little lemon juice. Sprinkle with parsley.

HERRING A LA FLAMANDE
For four herrings:
2 glasses dry white wine
1 shallot
2 oz. butter
juice of half a lemon
matso meal
salt and pepper

Melt the butter, add the chopped shallot and cook without colouring. Put the herrings in with the butter and shallot, add the white wine. Cover the pan and simmer gently until the fish is cooked. Add the juice of half a lemon. Lay the fish on a dish, thicken the sauce with a little matso meal, add salt and pepper and coat the fish with the sauce.

WHITEBAIT

Even experienced fish cooks, and most cookery books, define whitebait as a distinct species. They may be excused. Yarrell, the nineteenth-century ichthyologist, made the same mistake.

In fact, whitebait are the parr of herring and its near relation the sprat. The composition of the catch varies at different times of the year. In Sir Alister Hardy's great survey of life in the open sea, his conclusion is that whitebait are always a mixture ranging from up to ninety per cent sprat in spring to almost ninety per cent of herring in summer. You will never know the difference at the table.

In the Thames Estuary and the Wash enormous shoals are netted in their season from September to April. Never attempt to dismember the little fish when they are served. They should be eaten heads, bones, insides and all. The most nutritive parts of them are the bits which, in larger fish, are taken away.

To cook whitebait put them in a bag with some flour and make sure they are all covered. Put them in a frying basket and shake well before frying them for about one minute in smoking deep fat. Remove from the fat, drain well and serve on a napkin. Sprinkle with salt and serve with fried parsley and wedges of lemon.

HADDOCK

The élite of the haddock are the Arbroath Smokies, cured and smoked whole on the coast of Angus and Kincardineshire in Scotland. An admirable and important food fish, smaller than the cod, it doesn't, apart from the smokies, count with the nobility of the table. It is a fish which, these days, you lift out of the deep freeze.

HADDOCK MAITRE D'HOTEL
1½ lb. haddock fillets
juice from half a lemon
¼ pint cream
butter
salt and pepper
chopped parsley

Lay the fillets in a buttered oven dish and season. Moisten with the lemon juice and cover with the cream. Cover with foil and bake in a moderate oven for about 15 minutes, according to the thickness of the fillets. Garnish with parsley.

Haddock may be served in most of the ways recommended for cod. It is excellent for fish cakes, either fresh or smoked.

FISH PIE
1 lb. of cooked fish (smoked haddock or salmon are best.
   If cod or another white fish is used, add shrimps and
   some anchovy essence or chopped anchovies to the
   sauce)
1 onion
a little butter
½ pint béchamel (page 36)
½ lb. mashed potato
grated cheese (optional)

Flake the fish and cook the sliced onion in butter without letting it colour. Arrange the fish and onion in layers in a buttered pie dish. Pour on the hot sauce. Cover the whole thing with mashed potato and brown in the oven. This is a good dish to do ahead for warming up.

HADDOCK HONGROISE
1½ lb. haddock fillets
2 oz. mushrooms
1½ oz. butter
1 oz. flour
1 teaspoon paprika
½ pint milk
a few canned red pepper pieces or blanched fresh pepper

Place the fillets of fish in a buttered oven dish. Season. Add lemon juice, cover with buttered paper and bake gently for 10-15 minutes. Slice the mushrooms and cook them a little in the rest of the butter. Add flour, milk and paprika gradually to make a sauce. Add the fish liquor to the sauce, then the sliced pimento. Pour the sauce over the fish and serve.

HADDOCK MONTE CARLO
2 large smoked haddocks
1 oz. butter
½ pint milk
¼ pint cream
4 eggs
4 tomatoes
salt and pepper

Cook the haddock in the milk in a covered saucepan for about 15 minutes. Take the flesh from the bones, keeping it as far as possible in four large fillets and discarding the skin with the bones. Arrange this in a buttered fire-proof dish, slice the tomatoes over the top, season and put in a moderate oven. Reduce the fish-flavoured milk by fast boiling, and add cream. Pour over the fish and tomatoes and finish quickly in the oven. Arrange lightly poached eggs on top, either over or under the sauce. A little grated cheese may be added if liked.

SMOKED HADDOCK SOUFFLE
½ lb. minced or pounded smoked haddock
2 oz. butter
2 oz. flour
½ pint milk
4 eggs
salt and pepper

Melt the butter and make a roux with the flour. Add the milk and seasoning slowly, then the fish, and stir. Add the beaten yolks off the fire, and finally fold in the well-whisked whites of egg. Pour the mixture into a buttered soufflé dish and bake in a moderate oven for about 25 minutes.

Salmon, crab, or almost any other fish can be used instead of smoked haddock.

TUNNY

Tunny in this country comes mostly out of tins, the small fish which are taken in the Mediterranean and warmer waters. There was a time when it became a big game sport to fish for huge tunny among the ring boats netting for herring off the coast of Scarborough. But the big ones have now gone from our shores.

We must now regard the tunny, like the sturgeon, as only an occasional visitor. The canned tunny, which the French call Thon, is delicious.

SARDINES

Cans of sardines should be cherished like bottles of wine. By all means serve the less expensive, just as you drink the more popularly priced table wines, as soon as you collect them from the grocer. Nevertheless, even the most unpretentious sardine will improve with keeping.

The best sardines are a connoisseur's dish. A dozen tins of the most celebrated brands will cost nearly as much as a case of vintage wine. The most reputed of all—and certainly the most expensive—are packed by Rödel of Bordeaux (*Maison Fondée en 1824*). They come in a red tin with a silver medallion stamped in the lid. They are only available in England in luxury shops like Fortnum's and Harrod's, and not always on those exclusive counters. Recently, there were none available at all for several years.

Just as many famous vintages are now in short supply, because so many people are putting down wine as an investment, so the epicures are putting down sardines. But, if you want to start a collection in a more modest way, the best of the Portuguese sardines (brands like *Marie Elizabe'h*) are likely to turn out just as well with ageing as the more expensive. They are also more readily available.

Once upon a time the French packers matured the fish themselves before they put them on the market. Now, with increasing world demand, the most expensive brands are shipped as soon as the tins are sealed. Some of the packers are said to have a secret method of part-grilling the fish. But, if you want the old standards today, you must, as in so many other activities, do it yourself.

When you lay down a collection of sardines, it is a good plan to vary them as you would a selection of wines. You will then learn which develop best. Every tin should be labelled with the month and year in which you bought it. Connoisseurs claim that the best vintages for sardines coincide with the best vintage years for wine!

You should turn over the tins every subsequent month after acquiring them. This will keep the oil moving about the fish. After a few years, anything from three to five, the oil will melt all the bone.

At intervals you should add to your reserve to keep up a regular supply of properly ripened fish. Inside the tin they will keep indefinitely, and improve.

Never buy sardines which are packed in anything other than pure olive oil. Sauced sardines, or sardines in any oil less than olive, are plonk.*

WHITING

Whiting is the fish which you expect to find on the table with its head in its mouth. Commercially it is very important. It is open to question whether it is one of the best fish that comes out of our seas. Myself, I find it insipid.

I remember catching whiting in shrimping nets in my youth. My father to whom I brought them also found them uninteresting. But good cooks can perform wonders.

Treat them as you would one of the more desirable round fish.

MULLET

There are two varieties of mullet, grey and red. They both haunt brackish waters in river estuaries. The red mullet is generally favoured for its more delicate flesh. And connoisseurs prefer it with the liver left in, and sometimes with all its insides and scales as well.

---

* Alas, fresh sardines are not readily available in Britain. Those we get are frozen, which is not quite the same thing. In Brittany, the fresh sardines are one of the glories of the sea.

The grey mullet is acclaimed in the Channel Islands where great shoals move into the shallows on the incoming tides. Fishermen maroon themselves on islands of rock waiting for the fish to arrive with the sea, baiting the surface of the water with fragments of meat to tempt them to feed. Because the mullet has a small mouth and swims high, the fishermen dap for them with tiny hooks on the surface of the water. In England the grey mullet are not sought after so eagerly. Yet they are so thick in the mouths of rivers like the Test and the Itchen in Hampshire that they can be foul-hooked on a triangle spun fast through the midst of them.

MACKEREL

The mackerel on our coasts is less prolific than the herring; although, at times, you wouldn't think so. I have seen the breakers alive with them. I have seen the longshoremen throwing out a short Seine net and raking them in in their thousands. They auctioned their catch at about two pence a dozen, when two pence was two pence, on the low-water beaches.

The longshoremen weren't interested in eating them themselves. In Cornwall, that superstitious county, they told me that a mackerel with a white mouth had been feeding on drowned men. That is not true. The fish lives on the plankton, the most heathly organism in the sea.

What is fact is that the fresher the mackerel is eaten the better, preferably when all the colours of the rainbow are showing in its scales. But there are various ways of presenting it.

MACKEREL ANTIBES
For each person:
1 mackerel, filleted

$\frac{1}{4}$ *lb. leeks (white part only)*
$\frac{1}{4}$ *lb. tomatoes*
$\frac{1}{4}$ *lb. celery*
3 oz. butter
flour for dipping, salt and pepper

Melt 1 oz. of the butter, add roughly chopped vegetables. salt and pepper, and cover so that they do not brown. Cook the floured fillets in another pan with the rest of the butter. The fish fillets will be done in about four minutes. Place them on a dish, pour over the butter in which they have been cooked and arrange the vegetable mixture around them. Shallots may be substituted when leeks are out of season.

MACKEREL WITH OATMEAL
Mackerel are very good simply rolled in oatmeal and fried in butter.

GRILLED MACKEREL
For each person:
1 large mackerel
a little salad oil or butter

The fish should not be washed, but wiped as clean and dry as possible. Split down the back and brush with oil or melted butter. Season and grill gently. A good alternative is to wrap the fish in foil and cook in the oven, which will take about twenty minutes.

SOUSED MACKEREL
Clean the mackerel and lay them in an oven proof dish. Cover them with three parts vinegar, one part water. Add 12 allspice, some mace, bayleaves, cloves to taste, or a good mixture of pickling spices from a chemist, and some salt. Cook in a slow oven, covered, for three to four hours. Serve cold.

MACKEREL WITH SORREL (OR SPINACH)

Prepare the mackerel by removing head and tail and cutting down the stomach. Flatten and dry the fish. Melt a large piece of butter in a frying pan. When the butter is hot, put the fish in and leave to cook for about 10 minutes. Turn it over, but be very careful at this point as the fish is very brittle. Cook another 10 minutes. Add salt and pepper.

Remove the fish from the pan and keep it hot.

While the fish is cooking, wash thoroughly 1 lb. of sorrel. Put this in the butter in which the mackerel has been cooked. Make the sorrel into a purée but constantly stirring it. Let the excess liquid evaporate. Add one or two eggs and a large piece of fresh butter. Mix it very well.

Serve on a long flat dish and use the sorrel for garnish.

COLD MACKEREL (for hors d'oeuvre)

Boil together for one hour:
12 onions finely sliced
1 small glass of oil
½ glass of wine vinegar
½ bottle dry white wine
½ pint water

This is enough court bouillon for 10 mackerel.

Fillet the mackerel and put them in a baking dish. Pour the reduced court bouillon over them and cook for five minutes in the oven. Let them get cold and serve with lemon and chopped parsley.

COD

Cod is in both senses of the word, a common fish. I have taken it off the Lofoton Islands in Norway when,

to catch one in the long Arctic night, it is only necessary to sink a bare leaded hook to the bottom, and strike,
to get a fish. The migratory swarm was so thick on the
sea bottom that you couldn't miss. It was hard on the
hands, in the freezing saltwater, pulling them up.

It is important to tell that cod looms large in fish
fingers and fried fish shops. Anglers win silver spoons
when they catch them in British waters. In the Skager-
rak Race they leave them on the banks.

I am sorry to be rude about cod. They are full of
calories, and many like eating them. I have sat down
to dinner when a whole fish was served as the main
course. But cod, its name as dull as the fish, is not often
on Wheeler's menus.

Enough that the way of cooking the animal is the
same way that you cook its betters.

Coalfish (saith) is closely related to cod with a darker
skin. It is eaten like cod.

BAKED COD

Dip the pieces of cod in flour and put them in a
buttered dish with a knob of butter on each, salt, pepper
and a little milk. Cover with buttered paper, and cook
in a moderate oven for 30-50 minutes according to the
thickness of the fish.

GRILLED COD

Use tail pieces of cod if possible. Brush the pieces of
cod with melted or clarified butter and season with
salt, pepper and a little dill or garlic. Grill and serve
with melted butter.

COD FISH CAKES

2 lb. cod
1 lb. cooked potatoes
6 anchovy fillets (or bottled essence)

1 oz. butter
2 eggs
2 large onions
3 tablespoons chopped parsley
flour, milk and breadcrumbs

Poach the cod, remove all skin and bones, and mash until there are no big lumps. Chop the anchovy fillets and add to the cod. Cook the finely chopped onions in butter but do not allow to brown. Mix the onions, fish and mashed potatoes. Season with a lot of pepper and a little salt. Add the chopped parsley and the eggs, beaten enough to mix them. Form into cakes, dip in flour, milk and breadcrumbs, and fry in deep fat.

COD BRAGANZA
2lb. cod (for four people)
½ lb. chopped mushrooms
1 pint béchamel (page 36)
2 oz. fresh breadcrumbs
a little milk
paprika, bay leaf, salt and pepper

Poach the cod in salted water with a little milk and a bay leaf. Make a pint of béchamel and add paprika to taste. When the fish is cooked, remove the skin and bones and flake. Add the finely chopped mushrooms to the béchamel, then the flaked fish. Put all this into a buttered dish, sprinkle with breadcrumbs and put small knobs of butter on top. Brown under the grill.

COD ORLOFF
Cod steaks
½ lb. finely chopped mushrooms
½ lb. finely chopped onions
1 pint Mornay sauce (page 37)
2 oz. grated cheese

Poach the cod. Put the finely chopped onions in a pan with melted butter, soften them but do not let them brown. When almost cooked, add the mushrooms. Let these simmer until unwanted liquid has been reduced. Put the cooked cod in a dish and cover with the onion and mushroom mixture. Coat all this with Mornay sauce, sprinkle with grated cheese and brown under the grill.

This dish can be made the day before and put in the refrigerator. If this is done, it is important to put it in a low oven for at least an hour to be sure that it is hot all the way through. Then brown under the grill.

CONGER

This great ugly eel of a seafish, which can scale up to a hundred pounds, has taken many fishermen's fingers off in its formidable jaws when they were foolish enough to think it dead. The saying that a conger only dies at dawn or dusk may be biologically inaccurate but it provides a useful safety margin.

It is said, in the Channel Islands, to make a good soup.

SEA BASS

Bass, not to be confused with its American freshwater relations, is one of the most handsome fish in the sea. In its scaly silver armour, it is a perquisite of fine line anglers rather than a commercial product. It is said that bass should be prepared for the table like salmon, but the flesh is a little soft. Most of the recipes for dealing with it are designed to excite its flavour.

Cut in pieces, poached in a fish box, it is recommended that the stock should be supported with a little honey, chopped dates, currants, chipped almonds; and, surprisingly, served with a garnish of dumplings. This dish is called 'black fish'.

DOGFISH

Fishmongers call them rock salmon. Anglers call them tope. They are also known as huss, flake, rigg or nurse. They are, in fact, small English sharks.

They are quite edible and, if an angler husband brings one home, and skins it, it can be treated like any other form of whitefish.

HAKE

Another member of the cod family which is fairly scarce and usually more expensive than cod and haddock. Its best season is from June to January.

BLOATERS

These are smoked herrings, and very good too. They are smoked in Brightlingsea over oak chips. They are rare enough to be regarded as a collector's prize.

SPRATS

How well I remember the delicious sweetness of sprats when my mother cooked them as a tea dish when we lived on the Sussex coast. I wouldn't expect to find that unassuming fish on a Wheeler's menu. But I wonder what has happened to them since I was a boy?

The sprat is the poor relation of the herring (that's saying something in the current social scale) and it rarely reaches more than six and a half inches in length. Like Peter Pan, it never grows up.

It is collected in a number of small fisheries about the English coast. Brightlingsea is one of the places which is famous for its smoked and toasted sprats—home-smoked over burning oak-chippings in little wooden kilns at the bottom of cottage gardens. Fresh sprats require only the simplest cooking.

PILCHARDS

The pilchard, says Sir Alister Hardy, is really a sub-tropical fish and its range only just comes into our waters. In fact, the pilchard is a sardine of three or more years. In my opinion it is one of the good fish which comes out of a tin. Not to be compared with a vintage sardine, it is fishy 'plonk' which is entirely acceptable. Most of them are exported to Italy.

LAMPREY

I have never eaten a lamprey, that sucker fish of which King John is said to have died of a surfeit. I have never come across anybody who has.

VI

SHELLFISH

No question that British shellfish are the best in the seas of the world. Perhaps our temperate climate, neither too hot nor too cold, has something to do with it. It is interesting that in unusual frosts, our shellfish have been decimated; but they have always recovered. There are no shellfish anywhere else more tender and better to eat than in what Bernard Shaw called 'these misty islands'.

OYSTERS

I once had a present of a barrel of oysters which I fought for twenty-four hours. I did not know enough to open them. Certainly it can be difficult for a novice. Most of us are content to accept oysters, beautifully presented with a glass of Guinness or champagne, or both together as Black Velvet, in a fish bar.

During the nineteenth century, when oysters were a Cockney dish, so abundant that they were sold on the barrows for pennies, it was believed that they were an aphrodisiac. The barrow boys used to shout: 'Every one a baby.' There is no doubt that a dozen oysters make a man feel good; but, in the count of calories, they don't count. Apart from the pleasure of eating them there will be more ink in the pen from a fresh herring.

It is worth knowing how to handle the most delightful fish which comes from our shores. It calls for a strong hand. You need to use it purposefully with a pointed knife to break the hinge with a turn of the wrist at the small point of the shell. You should then insert the knife, three-quarters of its length, to release the muscle on the shell above and below. After that you have several options open to you.

Connoisseurs require that their oysters should be served in the deep shell or the shallow shell, or bearded. The French prefer that the green beard of the fish should be removed, leaving the eye of the fish in the shell. The English prefer an oyster in the deep shell with the marine juice all about it. There are those who want the fish turned over, when the muscle on both sides has been broken; others who prefer to suck it out of the shell.

Personally I have never eaten better oysters than those I ate at West Mersea with Bernard Walsh when we dredged them out of the sea and swallowed them like the Walrus and the Carpenter over a magnum of champagne. There is no doubt that, even after a short journey to London, the fish is not quite the same. The way to eat oysters is at the moment they come out of the beds. Few of us can achieve that.

It is not true that the larger the oyster the better it is. The big Colchesters are the most expensive. The middle-sized ones are the sweetest. The Portuguese relays, which are sold out of the English oyster season, are good too. The English oyster season, which many do not know, extends from August 4th to May 14th. The 'R' in the month is a little inaccurate. English oysters are best eaten fresh out of the shell, dressed with lemon juice, and perhaps a little wine vinegar and red pepper. But there are some cooked dishes which are worth consideration.

Note: no salt is added to oyster dishes, as oysters are already salty.

OYSTER SOUFFLE
6 large oysters or 12 small ones

2 *small whiting*
1½ oz. flour
2 oz. butter
½ pint milk
2 tablespoons cream
½ teaspoon anchovy essence
3 eggs
pepper

Skin the whiting, remove bones and pound or blend. Make a sauce with the flour and butter, add milk and the liquor from the oysters. When cooked, add the cream. If the oysters are very large, remove the beards. Dice the oysters and add to the mixture. Season to taste. Work in the separated egg yolks and the whiting purée. Whisk the egg whites and fold into the mixture, pour it all into a well-buttered soufflé dish. Set the dish in a pan of water and cook in a medium oven for 45 minutes. If liked, the soufflé can be turned out and served with a piquant sauce such as Wheeler's tomato and fish sauce (page 37).

A L'ANGLAISE
Means that when the oysters are opened, the muscles on both the top and bottom shells are cut, and then they are turned over.

A LA FRANCAISE
Means that when the oysters are opened, only the top shells are removed and they are left attached to the bottom shells.

FRIED OYSTERS
Bernard Walsh says: 'Just fry them like fish and chips.'

OYSTERS MORNAY
Allow up to a dozen oysters per person, depending on

size and how extravagant you want to be. You will also
need Mornay sauce, some grated cheese and plenty
of cream.

First make a Mornay sauce (page 37). Take the oysters,
live English natives, out of their shells and simmer them
in their own juices for a few minutes. Dry the deep-
sided shells and put the oysters back into them.

Add the warm juice from the oysters to the Mornay
sauce. Heat slowly, and when very hot add the cream.
Cover the oysters with this sauce, sprinkle with grated
cheese and place under the grill until brown.

OYSTER STEW (speciality of Bernard Walsh)
Shell the oysters. Melt some butter in a pan and cook
chopped shallots but do not brown them. Add the oysters
with the juice from the shells and a little milk and
simmer for 10 minutes. Remove from heat and add
paprika to taste and plenty of cream.

OYSTERS BERNARD
Open the oysters and leave in the bottom shells. Put
a knob of butter on each and sprinkle with chopped
shallot and pepper. Grill for 5 minutes.

OYSTER COCKTAIL
Open the oysters, take from the shells and put them
in a glass with their own juice. Add a sauce made by
mixing the following:
2 dessertspoons tomato ketchup
1 to 2 teaspoons horseradish sauce
1 tablespoon mayonnaise (page 39)
1 tablespoon cream

OYSTERS A LA POLONAISE
Open the oysters and leave in the deep shell. Sprinkle
with chopped parsley and chopped hard-boiled egg. Put

them in a warm oven for 5 to 6 minutes. Pour on some melted, lightly browned butter, and sprinkle with fried breadcrumbs. The oysters are then ready to serve.

LOBSTERS

The best size for a lobster is three-quarters to one pound. They normally reach that weight on maturity at seven to nine years. Like crabs they go into hiding to shed their armour and grow into another suit to fit an increase in their measurements. Big fish are favoured on gala occasions; but the smaller ones are sweeter on the palate.

When they are taken in the pots they are coloured a blotched green, sometimes almost black, varying their camouflage according to the sea environment in which they are caught. When they are boiled, ten minutes to a quarter an hour to the pound, they all turn red.

It is an old wives' tale that lobsters scream when they are plunged into boiling water. Death is instantaneous, and immediately all movement ceases.

The worst season for lobsters is June when they have shot their roe, and their flesh contracts. Connoisseurs like to eat them in early spring and late autumn. Their preference is for a hen lobster in roe.

The difference between a cock and a hen lobster is easily discerned. Like human beings, the hen lobster is broader in her tail. On his underside the cock lobster has tendrils which are hard and firm. There is no need to be particularly sensitive about lobsters. The fish is a quarrelsome animal with an unpleasant taste for cannibalism. Their Valhalla is reached with capers and the lobster pick on the table.

To dress a lobster, by comparison with a crab, is simple. A pointed kitchen knife should be speared in the fish in the hinge between the head and the tail. Driven home it is then carried back in an arc, through the centre of the fish to the tail fins. The line is clearly marked in the shell. Subsequently the head part should be split right through so that the two sides are exposed.

All that is necessary is to remove the green gut which runs round the rim of the shell. All the rest of the fish, including the jelly in the head, is edible. For cold lobster the fish is then ready for table with the appropriate tool to crack the claws and, if you are patient enough, the legs. For cooked dishes all the meat needs patiently dissecting.

BOILING A 2 lb. LOBSTER

Always make sure the lobster is alive and that the tail is firmly tucked under. If it is not it is a sign that the lobster is weak and perhaps will have very little meat in it when cooked. Also a lobster like that could be watery when cooked.

Get a large pan of boiling water ready and plunge the lobster in. Cook for 20 minutes.

Instead of water, you can use a court bouillon made with vinegar, a little salt, peppercorns, carrots, onions and a bouquet garni.

COLD LOBSTER

Cook the lobster and when almost cold cut in half and remove the bag and the black line which runs down the tail. Crack the claws so it is easier for people to handle, and serve with salad and mayonnaise.

Alternatively, *Lobster Salad*:

Take all the meat out of the shell and serve on a very nice salad with mayonnaise.

FRIED LOBSTER

Cook the lobster in the usual way. Remove the meat from the shell, dip in flour then in beaten egg, and then in fresh breadcrumbs. Fry in hot oil until a nice golden brown. Serve with tartare sauce (page 40).

GRILLED OR BROILED LOBSTER

Take a live lobster, cut down the centre and remove the bag. Put under a hot grill for 15 to 20 minutes. When cooked, serve with melted butter.

LOBSTER MORNAY

Cook the lobster in the usual way. Remove the meat from the shell and cut into largish pieces. Make 1 to 1½ pints of Mornay sauce (page 37). Put the lobster into the sauce and cook for 4 to 5 minutes. Put the lobster back in the shell and sprinkle with cheese, then put it under a hot grill until brown.

LOBSTER AU GRATIN

Cook the lobster in the usual way. Remove the meat from the shell and cut into pieces. Make one pint of Velouté sauce (page 36). Put the pieces of lobster into the white wine sauce and add 2 tablespoons of sherry. Stir continuously for 5 to 6 minutes. Put the lobster back in the shell, sprinkle with grated cheese and finish under the grill.

LOBSTER CARDINAL (Wheeler's way)

1 2 lb. lobster
1 pint lobster sauce (page 38)
2 tablespoons brandy
2 oz. butter
1 tablespoon double cream

Cook the lobster in the usual way. Remove the meat from the shell and cut into pieces about 1 inch square. Melt the butter and put the lobster meat and brandy in when warm. Flame the brandy and then add the lobster sauce. Stir constantly and cook for 3 to 4 minutes. Add the cream and remove from the heat. Return the lobster meat and the sauce to the shell and glaze under a hot grill.

LOBSTER CARDINAL (Escoffier)
Cook a lobster. When cooked, cut in half lengthwise.
Remove the meat from the shell and slice. Keep this
hot in a little cardinal sauce—1 pint of béchamel to
which is added ½ pint of fish stock and a little truffle
essence, reduced by a quarter. When dishing up, finish
the sauce with 3 tablespoons of double cream and 3 oz.
lobster butter (see page 41).

LOBSTER THERMIDOR (Old Compton Street way)
Enough for two people
1 1½ lb. lobster
2 oz. butter
1 oz. chopped shallot
2 oz. roux
½ cup fish stock
1 tablespoon chopped parsley
2 oz. grated Parmesan cheese
1 tablespoon double cream
1 level teaspoon dry English mustard
1 tablespoon sherry
1 tablespoon dry white wine
salt and pepper

This is done with a lobster which has already been
cooked. Cut the lobster in half. Remove the small bag
containing grit near the head. Take all the meat from
the shell, being sure to get the meat from the claws.
Cut the meat into pieces about 1 inch square. Lightly
fry the chopped shallots in the melted butter, but do not
brown them, then add the sherry, the white wine, the
lobster meat and the fish stock, and simmer for 3 to 4
minutes stirring all the time. Add some grated cheese,
parsley and the cream. Take off the heat, add the dry
mustard and mix well. Tip the contents into the lobster
shells. To the sauce left in the pan add a little butter

and the rest of the cheese. Mix, coat the lobsters with it
and glaze under a hot grill.

LOBSTER NEWBURG
2 ozs butter
½ pint double cream
½ pint velouté sauce (page 36)
2-4 tablespoons brandy

Boil the lobster in the usual way. Remove the meat from
the shell and cut into pieces about 1 inch square. Melt
the butter in a saucepan and add the lobster meat. Add
salt and pepper. Heat until the skin of the lobster is
a dark red. Add enough brandy to almost cover the meat,
then add ½ pint velouté sauce and mix well. Cook for
5-6 minutes, add the cream and just before it boils
remove from the heat. Serve on a bed of rice.

LOBSTER AMERICAINE (Wheeler's way)
1 2 lb. lobster

Cook the lobster in the usual way, remove the meat from
the shell and slice it. Melt 2 oz. butter in a pan with
2 tablespoonsful of brandy, and add the lobster meat
when hot. Flame the brandy, add 1 pint of lobster sauce
(page 36) or tomato and fish sauce (page 37) and mix
well. Cook the lobster in the sauce for 4-5 minutes and
serve on a bed of rice.

LOBSTER AMERICAINE (Escoffier)
1 2 lb. live lobster
3 oz. oil
4 oz. butter
2 finely chopped shallots
1 crushed clove of garlic
⅓ pint white wine

$\frac{1}{4}$ *pint fish stock*
1 sherry glass of brandy
1 tablespoon of meat glaze
3 tomatoes
2 tablespoons tomato purée
1 pinch of parsley
a little cayenne
salt and pepper

Take a live lobster, cut the claws off and cut the lobster down the centre. Remove the bag. Put the intestines and roe on to a plate, as they will be used to finish the sauce.

Season the pieces of lobster and put into a sauté pan containing $\frac{1}{6}$ pint of oil and 1 oz. of butter. Both must be very hot. Fry the lobster until the shell has turned red. Remove all the grease, sprinkle the lobster with chopped shallot and one clove of crushed garlic. Add $\frac{1}{3}$ pint of white wine, $\frac{1}{4}$ pint of fish stock, 1 small glass of brandy (flamed), 1 tablespoon of meat glaze, 3 small skinned and chopped tomatoes or 2 tablespoons of tomato puree, a pinch of parsley and a little cayenne.

Cover the pan and put in the oven to cook for 18 to 20 minutes. This done, transfer the pieces of lobster to a dish; withdraw the meat from the tail section and the claws. Set upright there on the 2 halves of the shell and let them lie against each other. Keep the lot hot.

Reduce the sauce to $\frac{1}{3}$ of a pint, add the intestines and chopped roe, together with a piece of butter the size of a walnut. Set to cook for a moment, then pass through a strainer. Put this into a vegetable pan and heat it without letting it boil. Remove from the heat and add 3 oz. butter in small pieces. Pour the sauce over the lobster which has been kept hot, and sprinkle with parsley.

LOBSTER NORMANDE (Wheeler's Way)
1 pint velouté sauce (page 36)
juice from half a lemon
2 oz. butter
¼ pint double cream
garnish
4 to 6 pieces of scampi
6 to 8 mushrooms

Boil the lobster and remove the meat from the shell.
Leave the tail and claws in one piece if possible. Make 1
pint of velouté sauce. Heat the lobster in butter but do
not let it brown. Add the velouté and the lemon juice
and cook for 6 to 8 minutes. When very hot, put the
lobster on a hot dish and add the cream to the sauce.
Pour the sauce over the lobster, add the fried pieces of
scampi and the mushrooms.

LOBSTER BISQUE
1 3 lb. lobster
1 oz. diced carrots
1 oz. onion
2 sprigs of parsley
1 bay leaf
2 oz. butter
2 tablespoons brandy
¼ pint white wine
salt, pepper, cayenne
¾ pint fish stock (page 35)

Cut into small pieces the onion, carrots and parsley
stalks. Add the thyme and bay leaf. Put into a saucepan
with the butter and brown. Cut the live lobster in half,
take off the claws, legs etc., put all in the pan with the
carrots and onions, cover with a lid and cook until they
turn red. Then add 2 tablespoons of brandy and ¼ pint

of white wine, and season with salt and pepper. Reduce
for about 5 minutes, then add $\frac{1}{4}$ pint of fish stock and
leave to cook for 10 minutes, after which remove the
lobster and take the head and legs off and put them back
in the soup. Put the soup in a strong bowl and pound the
head and shells as small as possible so it becomes a puree
and will go through a sieve. To this puree add $\frac{1}{2}$ pint of
fish stock, put on the heat and whisk all the time. Put
1 oz. butter in a saucer with 1 tablespoon of flour and
mix well, then add this in small pieces to the soup stirring
all the time. This will thicken the soup. Add as much
as is necessary—some people prefer it thicker or thinner.

Keep this in a bain marie until you require it. Put a
small knob of butter over the top to prevent a skin
forming.

Before serving, cut up the pieces of meat from the tails
into small pieces and add to the soup. Bring the soup
to the boil and add 3 tablespoons of thick cream, with
more brandy if you wish. Remember to remove the soup
from the heat when the cream has been added.

LOBSTER FLORENCE (Wheeler's Method)
4 oz. lobster meat
clove of garlic
chopped shallots
double cream
prepared curry sauce
lobster sauce (page 38) and rice

Saute the garlic and shallots in butter until brown, add
the lobster, season and flare with brandy, tossing for 2
or 3 minutes, then add a cupful of double cream. Leave
on low heat for a further 10 minutes or until the lobster
is cooked, but not overcooked. If the cream is thin, it
may be necessary to reduce it further by more cooking,
as the dish should be of a fairly thickish texture when

served. Pour into a cocotte, and serve with two sauce boats containing curry sauce and Americaine sauce respectively, and plain boiled rice as bedding.

CRAYFISH

Crayfish are lobsters without claws. The French call them *langoustes*. The French esteem them much more highly than we do. It is true that the tail is far more tender than that of the lobster.

Freshwater crayfish, which are common in all our clean rivers, are, surprisingly largely ignored in this country. They make a delicious dish and the French rightly think us mad for failing to fish them.

A crayfishing party, on the night of a harvest or hunter's moon, can be pure delight. All that is needed is the frame of an old bicycle wheel rigged with netting. The base of the net is baited with any over-ripe fish or meat available. You sink the net, preferably several nets, in the stream for a few minutes. In a good fishing area you ought to take a hundred freshwater crayfish in half an hour.

They are best eaten like prawns after boiling on a fire on the bank, accompanied with fresh cottage loaves and mayonnaise or farmhouse butter, and a bottle of Chablis.

CRABS

All crabs, even the little green ones that you find on the seashore, are edible. But they have too little meat to be worthwhile. The Bretons, who are much more parsimonious than we are, are fond of those ugly-looking creatures, the spider crabs. The only crab we eat is the red-backed one known as the edible crab.

Even that aldermanic character, with a white underside and black tips to his claws, is a fiddling fish to dress.

These days, a lot of fishmongers won't be bothered with the preparation of crabs, just as many of them will only pluck and draw game birds as a favour, at a price, for a regular customer. For that reason crabs are relatively cheap. Yet for those with the patience to unpick them they are amongst the best shellfish of all. As an end product the presentation of crabmeat in the upper shell, with an appropriate decoration of sliced cucumber and tomatoes and buttonholes of lettuce, can be one of the prettiest dishes on the table.

With their shells on, all crabs, according to size, look equal. But some are not nearly so full of meat as others. If you are selecting one from a fishmonger's slab or a seaside stall, look at the joint at the back of the upper and lower shells. During boiling the shell of a well-filled crab usually bursts a little. If the shell hasn't lifted, don't be satisfied until you are shown what is inside.

Crabs are normally sold ready-boiled. But, if you happen to collect a live fish on the seashore, immerse it in boiling water for about the same time as a lobster. If the claws have been left untied, you can handle crabs easily by spanning thumb and fingers across their backs. Alternatively you can draw their back legs together and lift them in the grip of your hand.

This is the way to dress them:

Ideally, you should have a wooden board and two plates, one for the white meat and one for the dark. You also need a utilitarian kitchen knife with a sharp point.

Twist off the claws and the legs. The legs of the crab, unlike the lobster's, are not worth saving. The claws, usually displayed on the top of a dressing, are as good as lobster's claws; although, of course, not as big.

Next, take the dismembered shell between your two hands, and break it open from the back with your thumbs. Even the biggest crabs split on thumb pressure.

When the shell is opened valuable meat, the dark

meat, will be left under the rim of the upper half. It should be carefully removed and put on the appropriate plate.

In the lower part a white core will show green ends which my mother used to call 'dead man's fingers'. They should be discarded. All the rest of the contents of the shell is edible.

The white core should be split and scraped into the plate put aside for the white meat. Anything you can dig out of the lower shell, after removing the 'dead man's fingers', is good.

If you are serving in the shell, the rough and ready way is to put in the dark meat first and the white meat and the claws on top. But you can employ any culinary artistry you like in arranging the meat with garnishing to taste. You can shred the meat fine, although I personally prefer it in larger pieces. But, of course, it needs to be shredded to make luxurious sandwiches for a crab tea.

DRESSED CRAB

Remove and chop the meat from the whole crab, as described above. The light and dark meat should be kept apart. Pack the meat back into the cleaned shells and garnish according to choice.

Lettuce, tomato, cucumber, chopped hardboiled egg, chopped parsley, are all suitable.

Make a dressing with mustard, olive oil and tarragon vinegar, or serve with mayonnaise. In either case, offer brown bread and butter.

CURRIED CRAB

1 lb. crabmeat
1 onion
1 teaspoon or more curry powder
1 oz. butter

¼ *pint fish stock (page 35)*
2 *tablespoons cream*

Cook the finely chopped onion in the butter. Add the
curry powder and cook slowly. Add a little stock, then
the crab in big pieces if possible, and more stock until
the consistency is right. Add as much cream as you like,
but beware of making it too rich.

Serve on a bed of, or surrounded by, plain boiled
rice.

CRAB SCALLOPS
8 oz. crabmeat (fresh, canned or frozen)
¼ *pint mayonnaise*
1 tablespoon Worcestershire sauce
1 oz. grated cheese
a little made mustard
buttered fresh breadcrumbs

Mix all the ingredients together and put the mixture
into buttered scallop shells or small flat fireproof dishes.
Individual dishes are more effective than one dish.

Melt some butter and stir in fresh breadcrumbs and
the grated cheese. Cover the dish or dishes with the
crumb mixture and heat under the grill.

PRAWNS (SCAMPI)
As I have said earlier, English prawns, the small sort,
are now a rarity. I am told that they are coming back,
those attractive fish which used to haunt our inshore
rocks. I hope so; but I doubt it.

There are some taken on the coast of Dorset; maybe
Ireland as well. What we get on the table are the larger
animals called Dublin Bay prawns, or scampi, which
come chiefly from Scotland, and the Mediterranean.

They are excellent to eat. They are mostly not our

own. I write with regret of what we have nearly lost. It is a pity that we now call them all scampi.

FRIED SCAMPI
Allow 1 lb. of scampi for three people.
flour for dipping
1 egg
milk
soft, fresh breadcrumbs
oil for frying

Dip the scampi in the flour, then in egg beaten with a little milk, and in the breadcrumbs. Deep fry for three to four minutes. Serve with sauce Tartare (page 40).

SCAMPI MORNAY
In this recipe use 8 oz. scampi per person
  Blanch the scampi briefly in court bouillon, cover with Mornay sauce as for sole Mornay (page 63).

SCAMPI WALEWSKA
8 oz. scampi per person
½ pint Mornay sauce
¼ glass sherry or marsala
1 lobster claw

Blanch the scampi in court bouillon, make the Mornay sauce, add sherry. Cover the scampi with sauce, add cooked lobster claw and glaze quickly under the grill.

SCAMPI PROVENÇALE
8 oz. scampi per person
8 oz. peeled tomatoes
1 clove garlic
1 dessertspoonful chopped shallots
1 oz. butter
flour for dipping

Dip the scampi in flour, melt the butter, add the chopped shallots, garlic and diced tomatoes. Add the scampi and simmer for eight to ten minutes. Serve with boiled rice.

SHRIMPS

The pink shrimp, now largely confined to the Wash, is the better. It eats like a small prawn. The brown shrimp, the sort which children catch in their nets on the tideline, is a fiddling thing to shell but, especially when fresh, delicious. They are best cooked for 15 to 20 minutes in seawater.

POTTED SHRIMPS

Shrimps are potted mostly in Ireland, but if you are at the seaside and have a good catch, this is what you could do:

Take 1 quart of shrimps, boil them for 8 minutes and then shell them. Melt 4 oz. fresh unsalted butter with a pinch of ground nutmeg and a pinch of cayenne pepper. Put the shrimps into small pots and press them down tightly. Pour the melted butter over the top and leave to cool. Serve with hot toast and lemon wedges.

SCALLOPS

They are properly escallops (*Pecten maximus*) a bivalve shellfish with a ribbed outside. They are usually sold on the half shell. If they haven't been opened, they can be dealt with by heating in water. The black parts and the beard should be removed, leaving only the white and orange of the fish. Their season is the winter period. There are many ways of cooking them.

All the recipes for prawns are equally delicious with scallops, but one must take care not to overdo the blanching or the scallops will be tough. To avoid this, slice the scallops laterally.

SCALLOPS AND BACON
Wrap each scallop in streaky bacon. Cook on skewers for ten minutes at medium heat. Serve with lemon.

MUSSELS
The season for mussels extends, with minor variations, from September to April. It is most important, although mussels are so abundant on our shores, that they should not be picked for eating without an assurance that they are pure. Pollution is now so widespread, purification plants are so necessary, that the charm of collecting shellfish like winkles, whelks, and even oysters, is full of danger. You would be better to deal with fishmongers who know where they come from; and how to deal with them. But, if you are assured of their origin, there are few dishes better than *moules marinières*.

Most mussels these days come from North Wales where the sea is cleaner.

MOULES A LA MARINIERE
4 pt. fresh mussels
¼ pt. dry white wine
3 shallots, finely chopped
sprig of parsley
2 oz. butter
¼ pt. cream

Mussels are one of our tastiest seafoods, but it is important that they be very fresh. The shells must be firmly closed when bought. Before you start to cook them you must wash them very well in several changes of water and scrub the shells, otherwise your dish will be ruined by sand and grit. It is also important not to over-cook them.

Take the chopped shallots and sprig of parsley, and put

them with the mussels in a saucepan with a pinch of
pepper. No salt, as this will not be necessary.

Place the ¼ pt. dry white wine and two cups of water
and this you must cook over a high heat. As soon as the
shells have opened and the liquid has risen from the top,
remove from heat. At Wheeler's we always take the top
shells off. This is not necessary but this way the mussels
are easier to eat.

Remove the mussels from the liquid and the liquid is
now your stock. Add the butter, the cream, and the
chopped parsley to this and pour over the mussels.
Sprinkle some more parsley on the top and serve.

MOULES A LA MARINIERE (as served in France)
Clean the mussels in the same way. Put into a large
saucepan, add the chopped shallots, a piece of parsley,
a bay leaf, thyme, and the white wine. Cover and bring
to the boil for 5-6 minutes. Strain off the liquor, put
the mussels into the dishes and add a little pepper and
lemon to your own taste. Pour the liquor over the mussels
and sprinkle with parsley to serve.

MOULES POULETTES for 6 people
6 pts of mussels
1 chopped shallot
parsley
pepper
½ pint of velouté sauce (page 36)
2 egg yolks
2 fluid oz. cream
¼ pint white wine

Clean and wash the mussels as for the Moules Marinière.
Put them in a large saucepan with the white wine, cover
with a well-fitting lid and bring to the boil. Strain off

the liquor and allow to cool, then add the velouté and reduce this sauce until it is like cream (single).

While the sauce is reducing, take the mussels from the shells. Here again, it is just as you like to serve them. At Wheeler's they are served in the half shell. When the liquor has reduced to the quantity you require, remove from the heat. Beat the egg yolks and cream in a bowl, then pour slowly into the liquor, stirring all the time. Pour the sauce over the mussels, sprinkle with parsley and serve hot.

ORMERS

These fish, with their beautiful shells, are almost unknown in England. In the Channel Islands they are rated as great a delicacy as the oyster. Normally they are only gathered in the long tides of summer. But, latterly, skin-divers have made a picking.

A large shellfish, about four inches long with a shape like a mussel and a shell lined with mother-of-pearl, it can be served in all the ways that shellfish can be.

VII

DESSERT

A book about fish cooking is only incidentally concerned with its accompaniments. This one is almost exclusively dedicated to the ways in which Wheeler's present their fish. But the subject extends to the desserts, and to the wines which enliven the fish.

There are many other books about the choice of wines. With fish they are obviously the white ones. Meursault, perfect. Chablis, or perhaps a light red at luncheon like Mouton Cadet. Black Velvet, Guinness with champagne, is excellent with oysters. Champagne, as an eleven o'clock in the morning drink, is the best beginning to anyone's day. I remember Lord Beaverbrook telling me that nobody ever came to harm through drinking noonday champagne.

There are dishes which are not in this book. I remember in my youth 'Sole au Père Monbiot', named after Monbiot, the restaurant manager of the old Trocadero. It was a *sole en broche*, fillets spun on a skewer interlarded with bay leaves and slices of onion. It was Monbiot who also taught me the perfect lunch to meet an overnight hangover. The menu was Bismarck herrings laced with Worcestershire sauce, followed by an entrecôte minute. The dessert he recommended and none better after a fish meal, was pineapple and cream, with a dash of Marsala.

Monbiot it was who also rightly insisted to me that the first sip of a glass of champagne is the one that matters. After the first sip the wine has a metallic quality. He advised, too, that before a dish of fish, you should run white wine round your mouth to coat your teeth. It gives an extra edge to the flavour of what you are eating. It is a tip which is rewarding.

In its early days as an oyster bar Wheeler's served few 'afters', except vintage cheese. Today, many restaurants in the chain have a large menu. Not the least of the specialities is the apple tart served at the Carafe. This dish is for a party of eight people.

APPLE TART (WHEELER'S CARAFE STYLE)

8 oz. unsalted butter
14 oz. self-raising flour
5 oz. castor sugar
1 egg yolk
$\frac{1}{8}$ pint of milk
4 lb. cooking apples and $\frac{1}{4}$ lemon

Peel and slice the apples. Add 3 oz. castor sugar and the juice of the quarter lemon. Cook gently until apples become pulped. Allow to cool. Make your pastry with the ingredients described above remembering to use only 2 oz. of castor sugar. Roll pastry lightly and using a large heatproof plate, cover plate with half of the pastry.

Pile on the apples. Cover with remaining pastry, trim and decorate edges.

Place on middle shelf of oven Gas no. 8 (450°F.) for 15 minutes. Reduce to Gas No. 4 (350°F.) for 15 minutes. Reduce again to Gas No. 1 (275°F.) for 30 minutes. Remove from oven at end of the final 30 minutes.

Fruit and cheese are undoubtedly the ideal culmination of a fish meal.

> 'Apple pie without the cheese
> Is like a kiss without the squeeze'

This book does not attain to tell you the heights of classic fish cookery. It tells you what will work, with the least trouble, in your own kitchen. If you follow it your dishes will be pretty good.

INDEX

Apple tart, 124

Bass, 12, 94
Béchamel sauce, 36
Beurre noir, 78
Black Velvet, 123
Bloaters, 96
Brill, 78

Carp, 57
Champagne, 123
Cod, 14, 91-4
    Baked, 92
    Braganza, 93
    Fish cakes, 92-3
    Grilled, 92
    Orloff, 94
Colchester oysters, 20-1, 26, 100
Conger, 95
Cookery of fish, 14-15
Court bouillon, 49
Crabs, 111-14
    Curried, 113-14
    Dressed, 113
    Scallops, 114
Crayfish, 111
Cucumber, 14
Culinary tools, 14

Dab, 61, 78
Dogfish, 95

Eels, 45, 55-6
    Pâté, 55-6
    Stew, 56
Essex bearded oysters, 26

Fish cakes, 92-3

Fish pie, 84-5
Fish stock, 35
Flounder, 78

Garlic butter, 41
Grayling, 57

Haddock, 84-6
    in Fish pie, 84-5
    Hongroise, 85
    Maître d'Hôtel, 84
    Monte Carlo, 85-6
    Smoked Haddock Soufflé, 86
Hake, 95
Halibut, 61, 74-5
    au Beurre Noir, 75
    Bristol, 75
    Poached, 75
Herring, 12, 13, 81-3
    à la flamande, 82-3
    Fried, 82
    Meunière, 82
Hollandaise sauce, 39

Lamprey, 96
Lobster, 103-10
    Americaine (Escoffier), 107-8
    Americaine (Wheeler's), 107
    Au Gratin, 105
    Bisque, 109-10
    to Boil, 104
    Butter, 41
    Cardinal (Escoffier), 106
    Cardinal (Wheeler's), 105
    Cold, 104
    Florence, 110-11
    Fried, 104
    Grilled or Broiled, 105
    Mornay, 105

Lobster—*cont.*
  Newburg, 107
  Normande, 109
  Salad, 104
  Sauce, 38-9
  Thermidor, 106-7

Mackerel, 89-91
  Antibes, 90
  Cold, 91
  Grilled, 90
  with Oatmeal, 90
  with Sorrel or Spinach, 91
  Soused, 90
Maître d'Hôtel butter, 40
Mayonnaise, 39-40
Mersea oysters, 20, 100
Mornay sauce, 37
Mullet, 88-9
Mussels, 117-19
  Moules à la Marinière, 117-18
  Moules à la Marinière, (French method), 118
  Moules poulettes, 118-19

Old Compton Street, 25-32
Ormers, 119
Oysters, 99-103
  à l'anglaise, 101
  à la française, 101
  à la polonaise, 102-3
  Bernard, 102
  Cocktail, 102
  Fried, 101
  Mornay, 101-2
  Soufflé, 100-1
  Stew, 102
Oysters and Wheeler's, 19-32

Pâté, eel, 55-6
Perch, 57
Pike, 56-7
Pilchards, 96
Plaice, 14, 61, 72-4

Diana, 74
Hamburg, 73-4
Portuguese relays, 100
Prawns, *see* Scampi
Preparation of fish, 13
Presentation of fish, 13

Restaurants, Wheeler's, 31-2
River trout, *see* Trout, river
Roux, 35-6

Salmon; 12, 21, 45-51
  Atlantic, 48
  Darne de Saumon Bernard, 51
  Grilled, 51
  Meunière, 51
  Pacific, 48
  poaching for cold, 50
  Smoked, 47, 49-50
Salmon-trout, *see* Sea-trout
Sardines, 15, 87-8
Sauces, 35-41
Scallops, 116-17
  and Bacon, 117
Scampi (Prawns), 114-16
  Fried, 115
  Mornay, 115
  Provençale, 115-16
  Walewska, 115
Sea-trout, 45, 51-3
Shallot butter, 40-1
Shrimps, 116
  Potted, 116
Skate, 77-8
  au Beurre Noir, 77-8
Sole, 14, 61-72
  Alcove, 66-7
  Antoine, 65-6
  Bonne Femme, Fillets of Sole, 70
  Capri, 65
  Cardinal, 70
  Colbert, 69
  Cubat, 68

Sole—*cont.*
  Dieppoise, 71
  Dover, 15, 22, 27, 61
  Dubarry, 73
  Egyptienne, 66
  en broche, 123
  to Fillet a Sole, 62
  Florentine, Fillets of Sole, 68
  Française, 72
  Gondu, *see* Grand Duc
  Goujons of, 71
  Grand Duc, 70-1
  Grey Witch, 61
  Grilled, 62
  Lemon, 61
  Maison, 64
  Marguery, 63-4
  Maryland, 67
  Meunière, 62
  Mornay, 63
  Normande, 64
  Palace, 71-2
  Pommery, 64-5
  Portugaise, 69
  St Germain, 65
  Scottish, 61
  Sovereign, 68-9
  Véronique, 63
  Walewska, 67
Soufflé, Oyster, 100-1
Soufflé, Smoked Haddock, 86
Sprats, 96
Stock, Fish, 35

Tartare sauce, 40
Thursday Club, 29-32
Tomato and fish sauce, 37-8
Trout, river, 13, 45, 53-5
  Brown, 53
  Rainbow, 53, 54
  Smoked, 53-4
  Truite au bleu, 54
  Truite aux amandes, 55
  Truite Cleopatra, 55
  Truite Grenobloise, 54
  Truite Meunière, 54
Tunny, 86
Turbot, 61, 76-7
  Fried, 76
  Poached (Hollandaise), 76

Velouté (white wine) sauce, 36-7

Walsh, Bernard, 15-32, 51, 100, 101, 102
Walsh, Carole, 15-16
Wheeler, 'Captain', 19, 24-5
Wheeler's, history of, 19-32
Wheeler's Review, 32
White wine sauce (Velouté), 36-7
Whitebait, 83
Whiting, 88
Whitstable oysters, 19-22, 24-6, 100
Wines, recommended, 123
Wysard, Antony, 30, 32